Panama

Panama

BY JEAN F. BLASHFIELD

Enchantment of the World™
Second Series

CHILDREN'S PRESS®

An Imprint of Scholastic Inc.

New York   Toronto   London   Auckland   Sydney
Mexico City   New Delhi   Hong Kong
Danbury, Connecticut

Frontispiece: **A Guna woman sewing**

Consultant: Michael L. Conniff, PhD, Professor of History, San José State University,
San Jose, California
Please note: All statistics are as up-to-date as possible at the time of publication.

Book production by The Design Lab

Library of Congress Cataloging-in-Publication Data
Blashfield, Jean F.
  Panama / by Jean F. Blashfield.
    pages cm. — (Enchantment of the world)
  Includes bibliographical references and index.
  ISBN 978-0-531-20789-5 (lib. bdg.)
1. Panama—Juvenile literature. I. Title.
  F1563.2.B53 2015
  972.87—dc 3   2014001863

1 2 3 4 5 6 7 8 9 10 R 24 23 22 21 20 19 18 17 16 15

Boats in the San Blas Islands

Contents

Left to right: **Jaguar, farmer, pollera, rainy day, marching band**

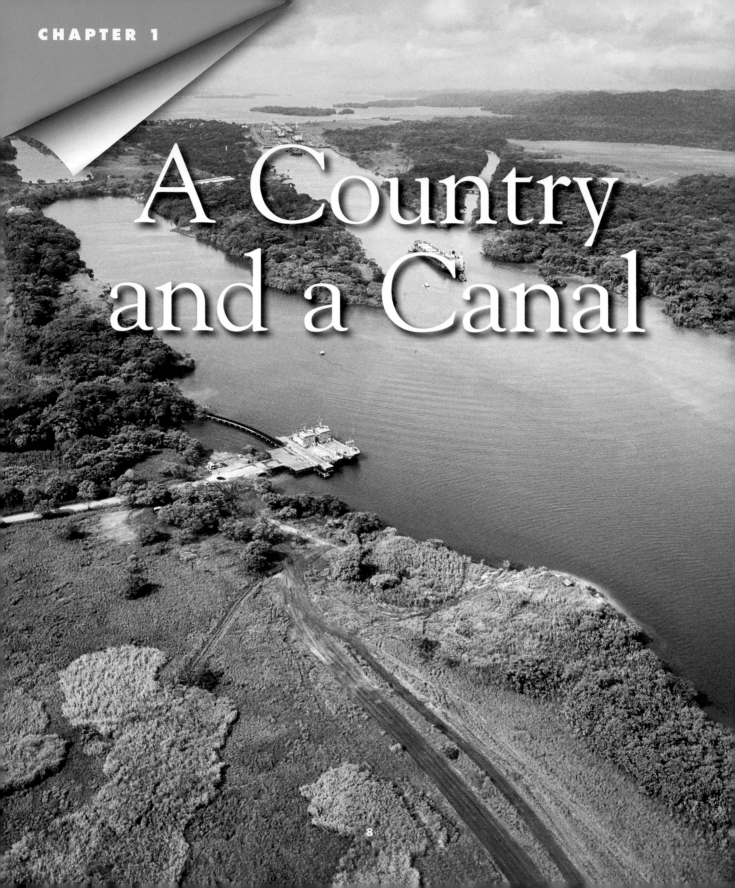

CHAPTER 1

A Country and a Canal

PANAMA IS A SMALL COUNTRY AT THE JUNCTION OF Central and South America. Because of its shape and location, Panama became the target of many people's dreams of making a water route connecting the Atlantic Ocean and the Pacific Ocean. Panama is the narrowest place where such a route could be made. At its narrowest, it is just 37 miles (60 kilometers) across.

Dreams of making a water route across the Americas date back centuries. In 1513, Spanish explorer and soldier Vasco Núñez de Balboa was trekking through Panama. He was curious about what lay over a rugged ridge of mountains. Indigenous, or native, guides led him and his soldiers through the jungle to the summit of the mountains. He saw in the distance an ocean that Europeans had not known existed. He called it the South Sea, but today it is known as the Pacific Ocean.

Opposite: **About fourteen thousand ships journey across Central America by way of the Panama Canal every year.**

Almost at once, talk began of the possibility of digging a canal through the narrow strip of land, or isthmus, that lay between the two oceans. That land was Panama. It would be several more years before Portuguese sailor Ferdinand Magellan found that ships could sail around the bottom of South America into the Pacific Ocean. But that was definitely the long way, so the idea of a canal through Panama never went away. To understand Panama as a nation, it's crucial to understand its all-important canal.

Starting a Canal

For most of the next four centuries after Balboa's discovery, Panama was not a nation. It was primarily a province of Colombia, which is located on the western shoulder of the South American continent. It was Colombian officials who, in the 1880s, gave a European company called the Panama Canal Company permission to dig a canal through the isthmus. They put Frenchman Ferdinand de Lesseps in charge. He had successfully dug the Suez Canal to connect the Mediterranean Sea with the Red Sea, opening a shorter water route between Europe and Asia.

The Europeans planned to dig a canal straight across the land, mountains and all, from sea to sea. American observers thought the canal needed a system of locks to take care of changes in elevation, but de Lesseps's plan did not include them. Nonetheless, many Panamanians were enthusiastic about the idea of the canal through their land.

Ferdinand de Lesseps was a diplomat for many years before overseeing the construction of the Suez Canal and the French attempt to build the Panama Canal.

By 1889, the Panama Canal Company had run out of money and all digging had stopped. Thousands of canal workers had died from disease and accidents. In eight years, they had managed to make a cut only about 12 miles (20 km) long. It left an open wound across the land.

The United States Buys In

The U.S. Congress voted to buy the assets of the Panama Canal Company, but Colombia, which had just ended a civil war, rejected the idea. Many Panamanians already wanted to rebel against Colombia, and Colombia's attitude about the canal added to their anger. The United States encouraged the people of Panama to believe they had the right to make decisions about their land and that they no longer needed to be part of Colombia.

What Is a Lock?

When a boat needs to travel between two waterways that are at different levels, a device called a lock must be used. The boat sails through a gate into a chamber. The chamber is closed to make it watertight. Then water is added or removed until the water level in the chamber matches the water level of the next waterway. The gate on the opposite side of the chamber from which the boat entered is opened, and the boat can sail on. The Panama Canal uses a series of three gigantic locks to raise ships up 85 feet (26 meters) and another series of three locks to lower the ships back to sea level at the other side of the isthmus.

Panamanians rally in support of independence in Colón in 1903 in front of a statue of Christopher Columbus.

Panamanians declared independence from Colombia on November 3, 1903. Three days later, the United States officially recognized the new nation. On November 18, the United States and Panama signed a treaty that gave the United States the right to build and operate a canal in an exclusive U.S. zone.

Panamanians had a nation. Americans were going to have a canal. Forever after, that canal would influence the nation the Panamanians had formed.

Oddly enough, no Panamanians signed the Hay-Bunau-Varilla Treaty, the agreement under which the United States built the Panama Canal and created the Canal Zone. The treaty was negotiated by U.S. secretary of state John Hay and Panama's supposed representative, a Frenchman named Philippe-Jean Bunau-Varilla. In fact, Bunau-Varilla represented the remaining French interests in the canal. He had also given money to support the Panamanian rebellion against Colombia because he knew that if Panama were independent, the United States would take over construction of the canal.

The Canal

In 1904, the United States started building a canal. At the height of construction, about 1910, at least forty-five thousand workers were laboring on the project. They came from

Panamanian workers shovel dirt during the American effort to build a canal across the Isthmus of Panama.

all over the world, joining the people from many nations who had earlier come to help build a railroad across the isthmus.

By the middle of 1914, ships first began traveling through the Panama Canal across the Isthmus of Panama. The center of the isthmus is a spine of mountains. De Lesseps had not figured out how to get through those mountains, but Americans used a lock system to help boats across. The set of three locks at the Atlantic end of the canal, near the city of Colón, are called the Gatún Locks. As a ship passes through these locks, it is raised to Gatún Lake, a huge lake that was created by damming the Chagres River. Approaching the Pacific, the ship enters the Pedro Miguel Locks, which has one chamber, and then the two-chamber Miraflores Locks, with a small lake between. The ship comes out at sea level at the Pacific end of the canal.

A tugboat passes through the Panama Canal on August 15, 1914, the day the canal opened to ship traffic.

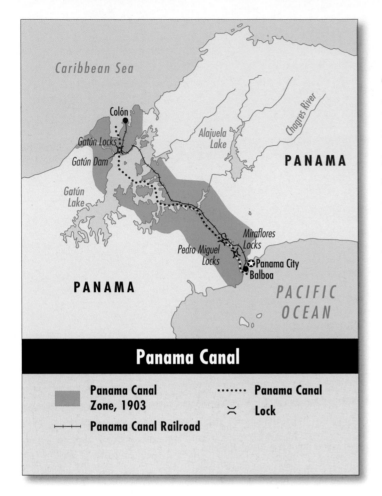

Panama Canal

Panama Canal Zone, 1903

Panama Canal Railroad

Panama Canal

Lock

The Canal Zone

For seventy-six years, a 553-square-mile (1,432 sq km) strip of land governed by the United States divided the nation of Panama in two. It extended 5 miles (8 km) on each side of the canal but did not include the cities of Colón and Panama City, even though they were close to the canal.

Within months of signing the treaty, complaints from Panamanians reached President Theodore Roosevelt. Panamanians feared that a separate nation would be established within their new country. Roosevelt responded, "We have not the slightest intention of establishing an independent colony in the middle of the State of Panama, or of exercising any greater governmental functions than are necessary to enable us conveniently and safely to construct, maintain, and operate the canal, under the rights given us by the treaty."

But that is indeed what happened. The separate "colony" of the Canal Zone was very different from the Panama beyond the Canal Zone's borders. The Zonians, as the inhabitants were called, were mostly West Indian and American. They lived in nice houses and had access to stores that people outside the Canal Zone were not allowed to shop in. The U.S. military was there to protect the canal, but the presence of the military often caused problems with people outside the zone.

Claiming the Canal

From day one, many Panamanians resented the American presence in the middle of their country. They also resented the fact that Panama did not receive much income from the

Theodore Roosevelt (in white suit) sits on a steam shovel while visiting Panama in 1906 during the construction of the canal. It was the first time a president visited a foreign country while in office.

canal. By the 1930s, frustrated politicians began using the slogan "Panama for Panamanians!"

World War II brought money into Panama, but the income disappeared quickly after the end of the war. By then, hundreds of thousands of Panamanians had moved to the two cities at the ends of the canal, and those cities quickly deteriorated from overcrowding and high unemployment.

Panamanian students march through Panama City in 1964, demanding that Panama be given control of the Canal Zone.

Throughout the 1960s, protests alternated with talks between the United States and Panama about changing the treaty. The talks led to several agreements that did not satisfy the Panamanians.

In 1968, Omar Torrijos, an officer in the Panamanian army, became the leader of Panama. He worked to turn world opinion about the canal against the United States. Finally, the United States gave in. On September 7, 1977, Torrijos and U.S. president Jimmy Carter signed treaties that would gradually turn the canal completely over to Panama. On December 31, 1999, the canal finally came under the control of Panama.

But Panama is much more than just a canal. It is a land of high finance and thick rain forests, a place filled with modern skyscrapers and ancient traditions. Panama has become a thriving nation at the crossroads of the world.

Gleaming skyscrapers tower over old churches in Panama City.

A Note on Spelling

In Spanish, vowels sometimes appear with an accent mark. In that case, the syllable with the accent should be stressed. For example, one of Panama's indigenous groups is the Emberá people. Without the accent, this would be pronounced em-BEHR-uh. But because there is an accent, it is pronounced em-beh-RAH. In fact, in Spanish the country name *Panama* is spelled Panamá, but in this book, it is written without the accent.

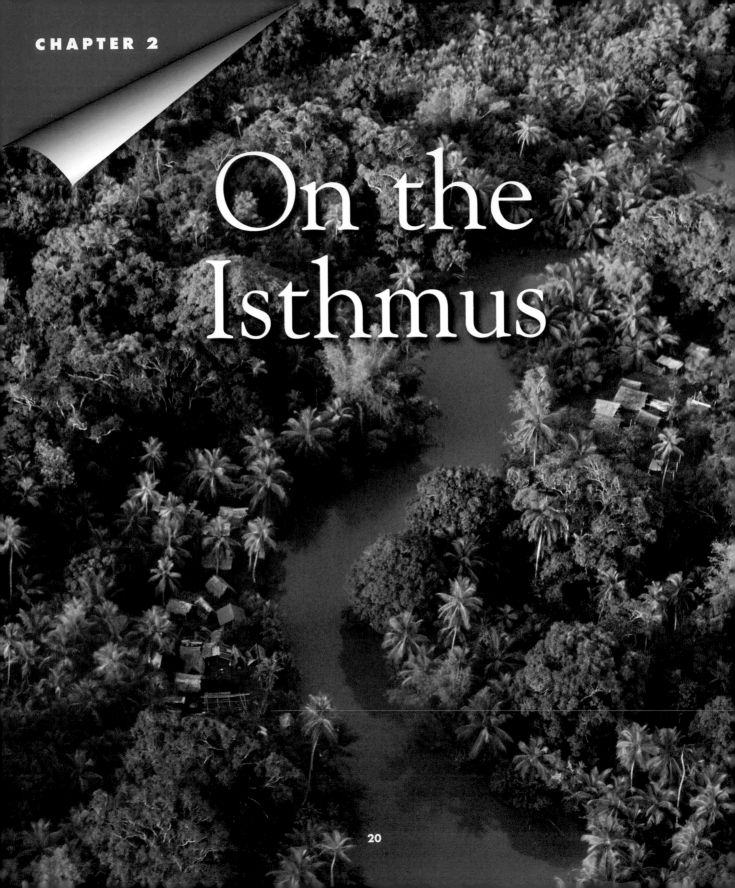

CHAPTER 2

On the Isthmus

PANAMA IS OFTEN DESCRIBED AS A BRIDGE CONNECTING North and South America. It lies at the southern end of Central America, south of Costa Rica and north of Colombia in South America. Because the Isthmus of Panama separates the Atlantic and the Pacific Oceans, it seems like it should run north to south. But in fact, it is shaped rather like a long S stretching west to east. The Caribbean Sea, an arm of the Atlantic Ocean, lies to Panama's north, and the Pacific Ocean lies to its south.

Panama is a small country, only 29,120 square miles (75,420 sq km). That is slightly smaller than the U.S. state of South Carolina. The isthmus is 480 miles (772 km) long and varies in width between 37 miles (60 km) and 110 miles (177 km). The narrowest part is near the canal, in the center of the country. The wider part of the isthmus, called the Azuero Peninsula, extends southward into the Pacific Ocean.

Opposite: **In many parts of Panama, boat is the easiest method of travel.**

Rising from the Sea

The Isthmus of Panama developed millions of years ago. Earth's outer layer is divided into many large pieces called tectonic plates. These plates are constantly moving in relation to one another. The Isthmus of Panama lies on the Caribbean Plate. In the Pacific Ocean off the isthmus are two smaller plates, the Cocos and the Nazca. A fourth, larger plate, the South American plate, lies to the south. This area is one of the few places on the planet where so many plates meet. Over millions of years, these plates pushed against and slid by one another. All this action gradually built up a land bridge connecting the two continents on the western edge of the Caribbean Plate. The Caribbean Sea occupies most of the rest of the plate.

As tectonic plates slowly collide, they force the land along their edges up, creating mountains such as these in Panama.

How Old Is Panama?

For a long time, geologists were certain that the Isthmus of Panama was formed about 3.5 million years ago. But in exploring the land being excavated to expand the Panama Canal, they made new discoveries that caused them to change their minds. For example, geologists found a fossilized tree that is 20 million years old. They also unearthed the remains of a tiny camel (above) that dates back at least 17 million years.

Camels evolved in North America and did not reach South America (where llamas, a relative of the camel, still live) until the Isthmus of Panama formed, connecting the continents.

So, how old is Panama? Ideas are changing rapidly. Unfortunately, many of the sites where geologists found important clues are already underwater and won't be explored again. Panama's age may remain a mystery.

Mountain Peaks

Panama's main landform is a spine of mountains that runs down the isthmus. The highest peaks form a continental divide, just as North America's continental divide runs through the Rocky Mountains. A continental divide is a line that separates rivers draining into different bodies of water. In Panama, rivers on the northern side of the divide run into the Caribbean Sea. On the south side, they run into the Pacific Ocean.

Panama's Geographic Features

Area: 29,120 square miles (75,420 sq km)

Coastline: 1,543 miles (2,483 km), including islands

Greatest Distance East–West: 480 miles (772 km)

Greatest Distance North–South: 110 miles (177 km)

Shortest Distance North–South: 37 miles (60 km)

Highest Elevation: Barú Volcano, 11,401 feet (3,475 m)

Lowest Elevation: Sea level along the Pacific Ocean

Largest Lake: Gatún, 166 square miles (430 sq km)

Longest River: Chucunaque, 144 miles (232 km)

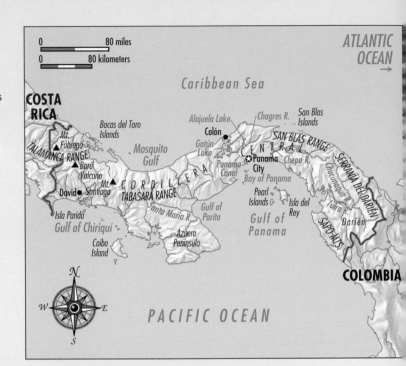

The mountains on the western end of the isthmus are a continuation of the Costa Rican mountain chain called the Talamanca range. These become the Tabasará Mountains. In the eastern part of the country is the San Blas range.

Panama's highest point, Barú Volcano, lies in the Talamancas, not far from the Costa Rican border. It is 11,401 feet (3,475 m) high. Barú is Panama's youngest major volcano. It last erupted about five hundred years ago. More than ten thousand people live in the valleys surrounding the volcano, and they would be in danger if the volcano erupted again. The most recent volcanic eruption in Panama occurred about 1620 in Veraguas Province north of the Azuero Peninsula.

Hikers who climb to the summit of Barú Volcano on a clear day can see both the Pacific Ocean and the Caribbean Sea.

Rivers and Lakes

Panama is a water-filled country. At least five hundred rivers flow through the tiny country. They run from the tops of the rainy mountains down to the oceans. Most of the rivers are not navigable because they are too swift or shallow. However, some rivers serve as the streets and roads for the people who live near them, especially in the marshlands of the Darién Province, in the east of the country.

The longest river in Panama is the Chucunaque. It is 144 miles (232 km) long. It is a tributary of a larger but shorter river, the Tuira. They are both in Darién Province. The Tuira is the only river in Panama deep enough to be traveled on by large ships.

Making Rain

In North America, most forests get their rain from clouds coming into the area. A rain forest, on the other hand, creates some of its own rain. Leaves release moisture into the atmosphere in a process called transpiration. In a rain forest, the trees are packed so densely that their green tops, the canopy, give off enough moisture to create clouds overhead. Those clouds then release rain, between 100 and 200 inches (about 250 to 500 centimeters) a year. The rain eventually soaks into the ground where the roots draw it in. The water makes its way upward to even the smallest leaf, and the cycle starts over again.

When many trees are cut down in a rain forest, that cycle is interrupted. If sunlight gets through the canopy to the ground, dense plant growth called jungle can grow from all that moisture.

The Chagres River, located close to the canal, was dammed in two different places, creating two different lakes: Alajuela Lake and the huge Gatún Lake. The upper part of the river is surrounded by Chagres National Park. The park was created to protect the flow of water into the canal system. It consists primarily of steep mountains and old-growth tropical rain forest.

Panama's largest lake, Gatún, was the largest reservoir, or artificial lake, in the world when it was created in 1913. It is 166 square miles (430 sq km) in area. Today, many larger lakes have been created, and Gatún is not even in the top ten in terms of size. The water in Gatún is used in running the canal locks and as the water supply for Panama City.

Islands

A huge number of islands are part of Panama. About a thousand islands lie on the Pacific side of the country and about six hundred on the Caribbean side.

Small islands dot Gatún Lake. Before the lake was created by the damming of the Chagres River, these islands were hilltops.

Ancient forests cover much of Coiba, the largest island in Central America.

Panama's largest island is Coiba, a crescent-shaped island in the Gulf of Chiriquí, part of the Pacific. It covers 104 square miles (270 sq km). Only a few of the hundreds of other islands in the Gulf of Chiriquí are inhabited. Gulf of Chiriquí National Marine Park protects the archipelago, or island chain, of Isla Parida, as well as many separate islands.

Closer to Colombia on the Pacific side is the huge Gulf of Panama, which contains an archipelago of about two hundred islands called the Pearl Islands. The largest, Isla del Rey, is Panama's second-largest island, which is large enough to have several small towns on it. The main tourist island is Contadora.

Two major archipelagos lie on the Caribbean side of the isthmus. They are the Bocas del Toro (mouth of the bull) chain in the west and the San Blas Islands in the east.

Panama's Largest Cities

Panama's largest city is the capital, Panama City, which had a population of 880,691 in 2010. It lies at the Pacific end of the Panama Canal. Within its metropolitan area are other large cities that could be counted as among the largest cities. These are San Miguelito, Tocumen, where Panama's main airport is located, and Las Cumbres.

David, in Chiriquí Province in western Panama, has a population of 89,442. It is the largest city that is not part of the Panama City metropolitan area. David is the most important city in the western end of the country. Officially called San José de David, it was founded in 1602. It is an important industrial city for Panama and the center of both agricultural and tourist activity in western Panama. David is an important stop on the Pan-American Highway, a network of roads that connects North and South America.

At the Caribbean end of the Panama Canal is the city of Colón (above). The city itself has only 78,000 residents, but its metropolitan area is home to about 242,000 people. When the Canal Zone existed, the city of Colón was limited to Manzanillo Island. But after the Canal Zone was turned over to the Panamanian government, the city limits were extended to many of the smaller Canal Zone towns nearby.

Santiago de Veraguas (left) is home to about 51,000 people. Located in the middle of the country, it is the gateway to the Azuero Peninsula. Banking is important in this city.

Climate

Panama has a tropical maritime climate. That means it has only two seasons, which differ in the amount of rain they receive, not in their temperature. January to May is hot and dry with pleasant breezes from the northwest trade winds. The remaining months are rainy and hot, with humidity usually near 100 percent.

The climate on the two coasts can be quite different. The Caribbean coast gets about 60 to 140 inches (150 to 355 cm) of rain during the year, distributed fairly evenly. The Pacific coast has a more definite rainy season, receiving about 45 to 90 inches (114 to 229 cm) of rain during that season alone. The Azuero Peninsula stays dry from December to April. The mountains, however, get much more rain from May to November.

Rainfall in Panama, especially in the mountains of the eastern end of the isthmus, is important because the canal operates

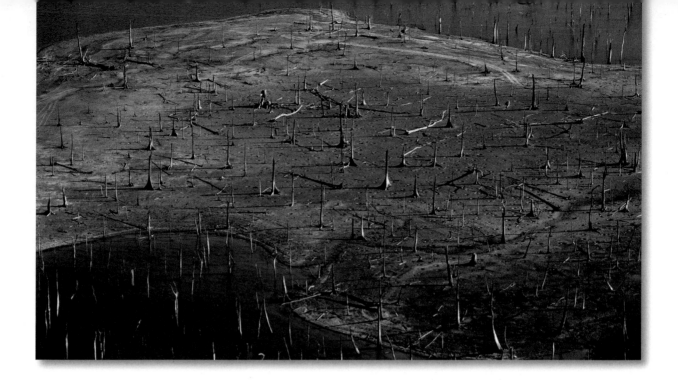

with that water. In a year of low rainfall, or drought, the canal can sometimes run into problems. Drought often occurs in those years when Pacific Ocean temperatures are warmer than normal near the equator. This is known as the El Niño effect. Several times when El Niño was active, there was so little water available that ships in the Panama Canal had to unload part of their cargo to keep from going aground at the shallow places.

When drought lowers the water level in the Panama Canal, it exposes the trunks of trees that died long ago, when they were submerged by water during the construction of the canal.

El Niño and La Niña

Every few years, ocean temperatures in the Pacific near the equator are warmer than usual. This occurrence is called El Niño, which means "the Christ child." People in Peru gave it that name because it usually appears in late December, near Christmas. Now the term is widely used because the warmer temperatures can affect weather all over the world. In Panama, El Niño can cause drought conditions, creating havoc with the water needed for the canal.

A similar period of unusually cold temperatures of the water has been called La Niña, the feminine version of the name. The colder weather causes more rain to fall than usual in Panama, and villages along the many rivers can flood.

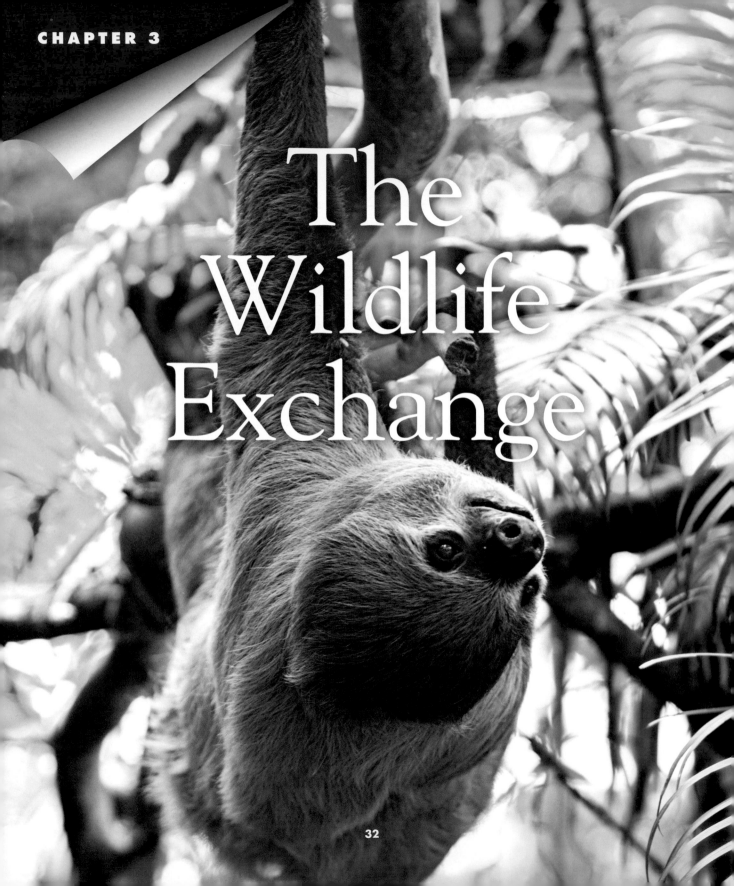

CHAPTER 3

The Wildlife Exchange

THE GREAT AMERICAN INTERCHANGE IS THE NAME scientists have given to the time when the Isthmus of Panama first connected North and South America, and living things from each continent were suddenly free to migrate into new territory. Scientists are no longer certain when that migration began, but it was at its height about three million years ago. Horses, camels, and saber-toothed cats, which had evolved in North America, moved southward. Armadillos and opossums moved north, as did gigantic ground sloths, which became extinct about ten thousand years ago. Because of the interchange, Panama has many more species of plants and animals than are usually found in such a small country.

Opposite: **Three different species of sloth live in Panama today. Sloths use their sharp claws to grasp tree branches. They go down to the ground only about once a week.**

Plant Life

More than ten thousand species of plants have been found in Panama, and new ones are being discovered all the time. About 15 percent of those species are trees found in the rain

Many trees in the rain forest provide support for vines, flowers, and other plants.

forests throughout the country. Rain forests often contain an incredible variety of species, called biodiversity. One study found more than 700 species of trees in just three locations. Some trees in the rain forest have many other plants growing

on them. These include the beautiful flowers called orchids, which thrive high up on tree branches.

Have you ever built a balsa-wood airplane? That lightweight wood comes from the balsa tree, or *Ochroma*, which can be found throughout Panama. It's especially common where rain forests have recently been cut down. Balsa trees grow quickly and die just as quickly. Less common than the balsa is the corotu tree. It is found out in the open in cities where it can spread. It has intricate compound leaves, and it produces bean-filled circular pods. Because of the look of the pods, it is sometimes called the elephant-ear tree. When these pods are dunked into water, they give off a useful soap. The canopy of a corotu may extend hundreds of feet across.

Workers harvest trees on a mahogany farm in Panama.

Some woods that furniture makers value most come from rain forests, and some of the rain forest has been lost as these trees have been cut. Loggers have been cutting mahogany trees for their beautiful dark red wood for hundreds of years, and now the mahogany tree is disappearing.

A very different kind of tree grows along the coasts. This is the mangrove, a type of tree that lives on the border between sea and land. Salty seawater is deadly to most plants, but man-

The jaguar is the largest cat in the Western Hemisphere. Jaguars live alone, with the exception of mothers and cubs.

groves can grow straight up out of it. The underwater tangle of mangrove roots serve as shelter and breeding grounds for many kinds of sea life.

The Big Cats

Panama is home to several species of big cats. The jaguar, the third-largest species of cat in the world, lives in both North and South America. Today, only a small population of these large spotted cats remains in Panama. Jaguars are important predators, feeding on deer, peccaries, and even alligators. They do not chase prey. Instead, they ambush it.

Another large cat in Panama is the puma. Pumas are nearly as large as jaguars and are tan in color. A smaller spotted cat is the ocelot, which eats monkeys, snakes, and rodents. The jaguarundi and the margay are other smaller cats.

Other Mammals

Tucked away in the canopy of rain forest trees are monkeys galore. White-faced capuchin monkeys, tiny long-limbed spider monkeys, tamarins, beautiful furry marmosets, and the very noisy howler monkeys are among the occupants of the high trees. These active animals usually just ignore the so-not-active two-toed sloths that tend to hang upside down on branches.

On the ground below the trees lives an assortment of other mammals. One of the most amazing is the giant anteater. This long-jawed, insect-eating mammal may reach 7 feet (2 m) in length and weigh 90 pounds (40 kilograms). Its massive claws

A giant anteater's long, sticky tongue can lap up more than thirty thousand insects a day.

can be used for tearing open the ground to hunt for termites. Anteaters sometimes walk along the pavement in small cities, ignoring passing people.

Other large mammals that live in Panama include the capybara, the world's largest rodent. It looks like a giant guinea pig and lives in groups both on open land and in forests. The peccary, a piglike animal, lives in herds in wooded areas.

Other, smaller Panamanian mammals include the kinkajou and the olingo. They are sometimes mistaken for monkeys, but they are in fact relatives of raccoons. The kinkajou can be a good pet if acquired when it is young. It is about the size of a small cat and eats fruit.

Three species of woolly opossum live in trees in Panama. These creatures have long tails that they can use like extra hands.

The rufous-crested coquette is one of fifty-nine hummingbird species that have been seen in Panama.

Birds

More than 950 species of birds have been identified in Panama. They vary from dull-colored wrens to bright quetzals with shiny green and red feathers that gleam in sunlight. Quetzals are found most often in the high forests of the Talamanca Mountains. Macaws, parrots, and parakeets add to the color in the sky.

Many colorful hummingbirds migrate by altitude—up and down mountains—instead of by latitude—to the north and the south. An unusually large number of hummingbirds live in the El Cope National Park in the center of the isthmus. Some of these tiny, flitting birds are found nowhere else in the world.

With its long coastline, Panama is visited by many seabirds. Some penguins make their way to Panama from the Galápagos

National Bird

Panama's national bird is the harpy eagle, the largest bird of prey in the Americas. This powerful bird, which has black feathers on the top of its wings and white underneath, lives in the upper canopy of the rain forest. There it hunts for prey such as monkeys and sloths. The harpy eagle has almost disappeared in Central America, but there are several locations in Panama where it is being protected. As the harpy eagle's rain forest habitat is lost, the bird will become less common.

Islands in the Pacific Ocean, 575 miles (925 km) from northern South America. Grebes, albatrosses, petrels, shearwaters, and pelicans all visit the isthmus. The most spectacular seabirds

A male frigate bird has a large red pouch on its neck, which it inflates to attract a mate.

there include frigate birds, some of which have wingspans that stretch over 7 feet (2 m).

Reptiles

Sea turtles live throughout the Caribbean, but their nesting sites are gradually disappearing. Four of the seven species of sea turtles nest in Panama: leatherback, green turtle, hawksbill, and olive ridley. Most of their favorite nesting sites are protected in either national parks or wildlife refuges.

Snakes are plentiful in Panama, especially at ground level, though they may climb trees, too. There are at least 130 species. The fer-de-lance has an X pattern on its back. Coral snakes are colorful, with rings of red, black, and yellow. They eat other snakes. The bushmaster is most likely to be found in undisturbed areas.

Baby leatherback turtles climb out of their nest and head toward the sea on Colón Island in Panama.

Unwelcome Wildlife

When the French first tried to build a canal through Panama, thousands of workers died from a disease called yellow fever. The workers were infected with the disease by the bite of mosquitoes, which carried the virus. Yellow fever gets its name from the yellow tone the skin takes on after the disease has attacked a person's liver. Cuban doctor Carlos Finlay first proposed that the disease was transmitted by mosquito bite. An American doctor named Walter Reed proved that Finlay was correct. As a result, Colonel William Gorgas of the U.S. Army, who worked as the chief medical officer in the Canal Zone, had mosquitoes killed along the canal route. This allowed the United States to build the canal with far fewer deaths than the French had experienced.

Today, yellow fever is rare, though it does occasionally strike isolated communities. Panamanians now are more likely to get malaria, which is also carried by mosquitoes. Malaria is particularly deadly to children.

The most frequently seen reptile is the green, or common, iguana. Found throughout Central and South America, it may reach more than 6 feet (1.8 m) long. Iguanas are often found on tree limbs near water. Though called green, these reptiles can vary in color.

National Parks

Panama has set aside about 5 million acres (2 million hectares) for national parks. This total amounts to close to one-third of the nation.

Green iguanas have a row of spines along their back. The sharp spines help protect them from predators.

The largest park is Darién, which is so wild it has almost no roads, just rivers for getting through the forest. The park protects the largest tropical rain forest outside the Amazon Basin in South America. But illegal loggers manage to find their way in and have been cutting down valuable hardwood trees.

La Amistad International Park occupies parts of two countries, Panama and Costa Rica. It is the largest nature reserve in Central America. Much of this park consists of cloud forest, where low-lying clouds lie at treetop level throughout the year. Because of the perpetual moisture, mosses cover almost all surfaces. The park lies in the Talamanca Range, a rugged, mountainous land where peaks rise to more than 11,000 feet (3,350 m). Parts of La Amistad are still being explored. In a 2010 expedition, twelve new plant species and eighteen new amphibian and reptile species were discovered. The park is

Hikers stand at the base of one of the many waterfalls in La Amistad International Park.

Towering trees are among the highlights at Soberanía National Park.

home to several big mammals, including jaguars and pumas, and Baird's tapir, a piglike animal.

Barú Volcano National Park surrounds the country's highest peak. The cloud forests on the slopes are good places to see the colorful quetzal. Cerro Hoya National Park on the Azuero Peninsula features many beautiful waterfalls.

People in Panama City who want to explore nature can go to Metropolitan Natural Park right in the city. With only a short drive, they can go to Soberanía National Park near the canal. Near the eastern edge of the canal is an area preserved as Camino de Cruces National Park. It provides a pathway for wildlife to move between Metropolitan and Soberanía.

Three of Panama's national parks are marine parks, two of them in the Gulf of Chiriquí. Coiba Island, Panama's largest island, was a prison colony for seventy years. The island was turned into a national park in 1991. Because it was used only as a prison for such a long time, the island's plants and animals, both of land and sea, remain relatively undisturbed. Humpback whales, dolphins, and hammerhead sharks often visit the waters. Gulf of Chiriquí National Marine Park, near David, is an important site for coral reefs, often visited by snorkelers. On the Caribbean coast is Isla Bastimentos National Park, an important nesting site for sea turtles.

Many colorful fish swim in the shallow waters of Isla Bastimentos National Park.

CHAPTER 4

Becoming a Nation

PEOPLE OCCUPIED PANAMA FOR PERHAPS TEN THOUSAND years before Europeans arrived there. There were probably several dozen groups of people living on the isthmus, but we know little about them, their history, or their ways of living.

These ancient people probably survived by fishing along the coasts and in the region's many rivers. It is known that they worked with metal. Archaeologists, people who study the remains of the past, know this from gold items they have found in Panama. The ancient people of Panama traded both north into Central America and south into South America.

Europeans Arrive

In 1501, a Spaniard named Rodrigo de Bastidas, who had been on Columbus's second voyage, decided to explore the Americas. He expected to find gold there, and offered King Ferdinand and Queen Isabella of Spain part of all he found if they granted him the right to explore what would later be

Opposite: **Centuries before the arrival of Europeans, people who lived in the Chiriquí region of what is now Panama created pendants out of gold.**

Rodrigo de Bastidas was the first European to set foot in Panama. He also mapped parts of northern South America.

called South America. He reached the eastern Caribbean coast of the San Blas Islands, which he claimed for Spain. That land was Panama.

Bastidas couldn't continue his explorations, because his boats were decrepit and unable to withstand further travels. That left the exploration of the Caribbean coast of Panama to Christopher Columbus, in 1502.

Other Spaniards followed Columbus. They were explorer-soldiers who came to be called *conquistadores*, meaning "conquerors." The conquistadores were motivated by God, gold, and glory. They believed they were exploring and conquering for God. Because they believed that spreading their religion would bring greater glory to God, they tried to convert the native people to Christianity. They had no respect for the religions and beliefs the indigenous people, or Indians, already held. The conquistadores also sought land and the gold and other riches it might hold, believing that acquiring land and riches for Spain would bring greater glory to themselves.

The Spanish conquerors enslaved many Indians. The native people were forced to work the mines and plant crops to feed the Spaniards.

Across the Isthmus

When Bastidas returned to Europe, his first mate, Vasco Núñez de Balboa, remained in the Western Hemisphere, settling down on the island of Hispaniola (where Haiti and Dominican Republic are now). In 1510, he established a settlement on the Panamanian isthmus, the first European settlement on the mainland in the Americas. He called it Santa María la Antigua del Darién. That region is still known as Darién.

Balboa did not yet know that the land he was exploring was an isthmus. In 1513, he and his party, made up of both Spaniards and native people, ventured southward, chopping their way through the forest. A few weeks into the journey, Balboa followed the instructions of an indigenous guide and climbed to the top

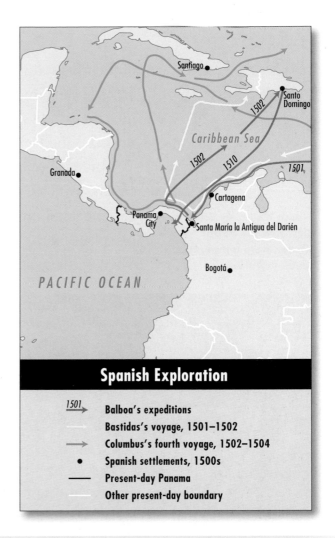

Spanish Exploration

1501 →	Balboa's expeditions
	Bastidas's voyage, 1501–1502
→	Columbus's fourth voyage, 1502–1504
●	Spanish settlements, 1500s
▬	Present-day Panama
▬	Other present-day boundary

Slavery in the Americas

The conquistadores forced many indigenous people in the Americas into slavery. Hundreds of thousands of Indians soon died from European diseases. They had never before been exposed to these diseases, so their bodies had no natural resistance to them. So many Indians died that the conquerors were running out of people to do the work for them. African slaves may have been in Panama as early as 1510, but it wasn't until 1517 that Spain's King Charles V began giving contracts for Europeans to supply African slaves to the American colonies. That began the transatlantic slave trade that soon included North America and the British colonies there. The slave trade lasted more than three hundred years.

of the mountains. There, in the distance, he saw an ocean. He and a few excited men swarmed down to the shore and walked into the sea. He claimed this new "South Sea" in the name of Spain's King Ferdinand.

Panama became the center of all exploration for the Spanish crown. In 1519, the king's governor left Darién and established a new capital on the Pacific coast. It became Panama City, the first place on the Pacific Ocean coast to be settled by Europeans. Many settlements and trade routes followed.

Vasco Núñez de Balboa first saw the Pacific Ocean from a mountain peak in Darién.

The indigenous people of Panama did not welcome the Spanish soldiers. A few helped the invaders, but most rebelled at being forced into slavery.

Urracá was a leader of the Guaymí people in the early sixteenth century. He worked with other indigenous leaders to help defeat the Spanish. Once he was captured, but he escaped and continued his fight against the conquistadores. Urracá's image is on the centesimo coin, the smallest Panamanian coin.

Bayano was a black slave brought to Panama, probably from Africa. He led a rebellion of enslaved people who escaped into the jungle of Darién. They set up their own community. The Spanish colonial governor later captured Bayano and sent him to Spain, where he died.

In 1534, King Charles V set his engineers to planning a canal through the isthmus. It would be almost four hundred years before that canal was realized.

Treasure

Panama remained a Spanish possession for the next three hundred years. Gold, silver, and other treasure the Spanish collected in South America flowed out of Panama. Other European nations decided they wanted some, too, so they sent in pirates. The English and French took several Caribbean islands, including Jamaica, from Spain. They used the islands as bases for attacking Spanish ships sailing from Panama. Sir Francis Drake sailed for the English queen Elizabeth. He took vast amounts of treasure back to Britain.

British pirate Henry Morgan and the men from thirty-six ships attacked and burned Panama City.

In 1670, Spain and England reached an agreement that they would no longer attack each other, but pirate Henry Morgan paid no attention. The next year, sailing with a huge number of English and French ships, he attacked Panama City. He stole everything he could and then burned the city. The Panamanians quickly rebuilt their capital a few miles away in a location that was easier to defend.

Forgotten Panama

As less and less silver from South American mines was transported through Panama, Panama became less important to Spain. Not even the pirates were drawn there anymore. Over time, Spain seemed to forget about Panama.

Not everyone forgot it, however. The French suggested to Spain that they build a canal. Panamanians suggested to the British that they would be welcomed if they came to build a canal. Even U.S. president Thomas Jefferson considered a canal a good idea. At the time, though, the canal did not get built.

Revolution

As Latin American countries began to see themselves as more and more separate from Spain, the criollos (Spanish people born in the Western Hemisphere) began to talk about taking charge of their own countries.

Back in Spain, the royal family lost their own country when the French emperor Napoleon sent his army in conquest in 1808. When word of the change in Spanish rule reached them, Latin American revolutionaries took the opportunity for revolt against the colonial power. Simón Bolívar, who came to be called the Liberator, formed a new nation, Gran Colombia, which covered all of northern South America.

During these years, people in Panama began to have a sense of their own identity. Called *panameñidad*, it was a feeling of being Panamanian instead of being Spanish. Finally, on November 28, 1821, the Panamanians declared their independence from Spain. They immediately chose to join Gran Colombia. It was the first time they had made such a choice on their own.

Gran Colombia, 1824

—— Present-day boundaries

For the next decades, Panama's history was Colombia's history, though leaders in Bogotá tended to ignore the people in the distant isthmus. Then, suddenly, Panama became significant again, perhaps not to Colombia but to the United States.

The Quest for Treasure Returns

In 1848, the California Gold Rush started. People from all over the world raced to California to start digging for gold. There was not yet a railroad across the United States. To get from the East Coast to California, the Forty-Niners, as the

Future gold prospectors crowded onto ships to join the California Gold Rush. The journey by sea from New York City around the tip of South America and north to San Francisco, California, took about six months.

The Panama Canal Railroad ran 47 miles (76 km) across the Isthmus of Panama.

gold-seekers came to be called, had to travel by wagon across the vast continent, take a ship around South America, or somehow make their way across the Isthmus of Panama.

It was the U.S. Post Office that pushed for improving transportation in Panama. The post office sent mail from the East Coast to Panama, and from Panama to the West Coast, but something had to link the two sides of the isthmus. American businesspeople agreed to build a railroad across the narrow but treacherous land. It took five years and several thousand lives, but the railroad was completed by 1855. Business boomed in Panama. Until a railroad across the United States was completed fourteen years later, the journey across Panama was the easiest way to get from the East to the goldfields of California.

During those years, rebels became active in Panama. Chaos grew, and the government in Colombia invited the United

Colón was quickly rebuilt after being burned to the ground in 1885.

States to send military forces to calm things down, but they did not arrive in time to stop the city of Colón from burning down. More troops guarded the all-important railroad, to keep it from being destroyed.

Digging and Death

The railroad was very useful, but the United States wanted to replace it with a canal. So did Europeans, who wanted an easier way to reach their colonies and trading partners in the Pacific. The Suez Canal in Egypt demonstrated the advantage a waterway had over a railroad. After this canal opened in 1869, ships had a much shorter route to travel from Europe to Asia. Ferdinand de Lesseps had overseen the construction of the Suez Canal. Ten years later, de Lesseps formed the Panama Canal Company to build a canal across the Isthmus of Panama.

De Lesseps didn't know much about Panama. He had not realized how much digging through wet rain forest differed from digging through the dry land of North Africa. Nor could he have predicted that, in Panama, disease would kill workers faster than accidents. French workers began digging the canal in 1881. During the eight years that they worked at this site, at least twenty thousand of the workers died.

In 1889, the French canal company went bankrupt. All work stopped. But the United States still wanted a canal. American officials went to the government of Colombia and proposed that the Americans build one.

France used steam-powered excavators to remove dirt from the proposed canal site.

Trouble in Colombia

During this time, Colombia was busy with its own problems. Panama was still part of Colombia, so it was deeply involved in these troubles. From 1899 to 1902, Colombians fought each other in the Thousand Days' War. They fought over election fraud, a failing economy, and who had the right to govern. More than one hundred thousand Colombians died during that war. Toward the end of the war, most of the fighting took place in Panama.

Colombians battled each other during the Thousand Days' War.

The United States started a war with Spain in 1898. The Spanish-American War led to the United States acquiring the Philippines in the Pacific Ocean, and Puerto Rico and Cuba in the Atlantic. The United States was now a world power, and safe passage across the isthmus was vital.

One group in the United States was determined to build a canal across Nicaragua, north of Panama. Another group insisted that the canal cross Panama. Those pushing

for Panama won. It was time to go to Colombia to request the right to build the canal.

Good-bye Colombia

As part of Colombia, Panamanians had long felt ignored and been unhappy as Colombians. They often talked of breaking away. When the Colombian Senate in Bogotá refused to ratify, or approve, the Panama Canal Treaty with the United States, it was time to act. At the urging of the Americans, the Municipal Council of the District of Panama declared its independence from Colombia on November 3, 1903. The declaration emphasized the fact that the people of the isthmus had benefited little from being part of Colombia.

The U.S. Navy routed Spanish forces in July 1898 at the Battle of Santiago, Cuba, the largest battle of the Spanish-American War. Spain would soon surrender Cuba, the Philippines, and other lands to the United States.

The Man Who Built the Canal

U.S. president Theodore Roosevelt put George Washington Goethals (right) in charge of building the Panama Canal. He was an army officer and engineer who had built bridges and other canals in the United States. Often called the Czar of Panama, he knew how to direct the project and would let nothing stand in his way. He succeeded in completing the canal two years ahead of schedule.

On November 6, the United States officially recognized the new Republic of Panama. In the coming months, European nations would also recognize the Republic of Panama. Colombia did not recognize Panama as an independent nation until 1921.

An American ship, the SS *Ancon*, made the first official transit of the Panama Canal in a ceremony on August 15, 1914. The ship was named after the Panamanian township where the Canal Commission was headquartered. Much work remained to be done on the canal, however, and it did not open for routine business until 1920.

Opposition

Finally independent of Colombia, Panama next had to contend with U.S. control of part of its nation. An estimated 12 percent of Panamanians worked in the Canal Zone, and in the years after the canal opened, much of the political activity in Panama was built around resentment against the United States for interfering in the lives of the Panamanians.

In 1936, the United States and Panama signed a treaty that ended the right of the United States to interfere in Panamanian life and government. It also decreed that the United States had no right to have military bases in Panama that were outside the Canal Zone. Yet during World War II, the U.S. military occupied several sites within Panama because they considered it vitally important to protect the canal.

Arnulfo Arias was elected president of Panama in 1940, during the early years of World War II. He demanded huge

In 1939, U.S. troops stationed in Panama stand guard over a large gun trained on the sea. The United States was determined to protect the Panama Canal during World War II.

payments from the United States for the use of the sites outside the Canal Zone. After the war, the United States wanted to keep using all those sites outside the Canal Zone. When the Panamanian government agreed, thousands of Panamanians protested. The National Assembly refused to ratify the new treaty. Opposition to the U.S. presence in Panama was building.

The Day of the Martyrs

In 1958, Panamanian students, frustrated with the U.S. presence in their country, entered the Canal Zone to plant Panama's flag. U.S. soldiers and Panama's own National Guard attacked the students. The anger boiled until, in 1963, U.S. president John F. Kennedy agreed that within the Canal Zone, the Panamanian flag could fly alongside the American flag except at military sites. A bitter battle broke out between Panamanians and Zonians, who did not want the Panamanian flag to fly in their territory. The governor of the Canal Zone eventually decreed that the U.S. flag would no longer be flown at nonmilitary sites, such as schools and post offices. That meant that the Panamanian flag could not be flown either.

The following January, in 1964, some very conservative Zonians rebelled. Students starting flying the American flag at their schools. Students at Balboa High School camped out by their flagpole to prevent the flag from being removed. This turned into a battle between Panamanian and Zonian high school students, especially when a Panamanian flag was torn. Then, a student—one who was not even protesting—was killed by the police. He became the first of what were called the Martyrs. The violence spread, and the American military took command of the Canal Zone.

Many businesses and government buildings in Panama City were set on fire. Some Panamanians died in the fires. One eleven-year-old girl, standing outside on a balcony, was shot and killed.

After three days, the violence ended. Altogether twenty-one Panamanians and four U.S. soldiers had died. January 9

High school students fight with Canal Zone police over a torn Panamanian flag on January 9, 1964.

Life in the Canal Zone

For about sixty years, the people who lived in the Canal Zone—the engineers, skilled workers, and executives—had a very different life from the Panamanians elsewhere in the country. The Canal Commission wanted to keep the employees content so that they would stay. They had free housing and were given many of the luxuries that let them live like well-to-do Americans in the United States. The children went to excellent schools and could shop at good stores filled with inexpensive products from the north. The Panamanians who lived outside the Canal Zone were not allowed to shop in those stores. The Zonians had plenty of places to relax as well. They had access to great beaches, golf courses, bowling alleys, baseball fields, movies, and dances. When the Canal Zone was disestablished, the Panamanians gradually moved in, expanding their cities. Former military bases became new subdivisions.

has since been recognized as Martyrs' Day. The events of 1964 were a factor in the United States transferring control of the Canal Zone to Panama.

Time of Dictators

Arnulfo Arias was again in charge in 1968 when the Panamanian military, led by Colonel Omar Torrijos, forcibly took over the government because Arias planned to change the structure of the military. This began twenty-one years of military dictatorship in Panama. A new constitution was written that gave Torrijos unlimited power.

Meanwhile, Panamanians continued to object to the U.S. involvement in their country and their lives. On September

7, 1977, U.S. President Jimmy Carter and Torrijos signed a treaty that cancelled the 1903 treaty and gradually turned the canal over to the Panamanians. As of midnight on December 31, 1999, Panama would take total control of their canal. An additional treaty also guaranteed that the canal, when it was fully under Panamanian control, would be forever neutral in the event of war and that the United States would keep the right to defend the canal. Two-thirds of the Panamanian people voted in favor of the treaties.

In 1981, Torrijos died in a plane crash, and a little-known general named Manuel Noriega took control. Noriega encouraged an economy based on the passage of illegal drugs from Colombia, through Panama, and on into the United States. He also terrorized opponents and refused to accept the results of elections. After a while, U.S. officials decided they needed to try to end Noriega's rule.

President Jimmy Carter (left) shakes hands with Omar Torrijos at the signing of the Panama Canal Treaty.

In 1989, a U.S. soldier was killed in Panama, and the United States used the murder as an excuse to send in troops to capture Noriega. The military removed Noriega from power and took him to the United States to be tried on drug and money laundering charges. Several hundred Panamanians died during the invasion. Noriega was tried in a Florida court, convicted, and sentenced to prison. He eventually served seventeen years and was then taken to France, where he was tried again for money laundering and imprisoned for several years. Finally, he was released and sent back to Panama. He is still serving time in a Panamanian prison for crimes he carried out while he was in power.

Buildings in Panama City burn during the U.S. invasion of Panama in 1989.

Owning Their Canal

With Noriega gone, the new president, Guillermo Endara, transformed the military into a civilian police force and worked toward Panama's economic recovery. The nation's first female president, Mireya Moscoso, the widow of Arnulfo Arias, was in charge when the canal was completely turned over to Panama.

In 2004, President Martín Torrijos, the son of the former dictator, was elected president. He supported a proposal to expand the canal by adding more and bigger locks and dredging portions of the canal, making it deeper. The people of the country voted in favor of the $5 billion project in 2006. They were on their way to deciding their own destiny. The expanded canal will likely open in 2016. Panama's future will depend on the newer and larger Panama Canal.

Mireya Moscoso served as president of Panama from 1999 to 2004.

CHAPTER 5

Governing Panama

PANAMA'S CURRENT CONSTITUTION IS THE FOURTH one in its history. This constitution was written during the dictatorship of Omar Torrijos and took effect on October 11, 1972. Because the 1972 version of the constitution gave the military great power, it has since been amended, or changed, several times. Today, Panama is a constitutional democracy. Its capital is Panama City, which is also the largest city.

Everyone who is at least eighteen years old is eligible to vote. Although, officially, people are required to vote, there are no penalties if people do not vote. In recent years, between 75 and 80 percent of eligible voters have gone to the polls in national elections. Some women in Panama have had the right to vote since 1941, and all women gained the right to vote in 1946.

Executive Branch

Like the United States, Panama's government is divided into three branches: the executive, the legislative, and the judicial.

Opposite: **President Ricardo Martinelli gives a speech before the National Assembly. In addition to his work in government, Martinelli is a successful businessperson.**

Celebrating Independence

Americans may have the Fourth of July, but Panamanians have an entire month devoted to celebrating their independence. November includes four national days, when schools are closed and people celebrate with fireworks, music in the streets, and parades.

November 3: Independence Day. On this day in 1903, Panama broke away from Colombia and became a separate republic.

November 4: Flag Day

November 10: First Cry for Independence Day. On this day in 1821, in the village of La Villa de los Santos, leaders first issued a call for independence from Spain.

November 28: Independence from Spain Day. On this day in 1821, Panama declared its independence from Spain.

The president is the head of the executive branch. The president and the vice president are elected by popular vote to five-year terms. The president may serve only one term and then must wait for ten years before running for the position again. Until 2009, there were two vice presidents. Then the constitution was amended, and now there is only one.

In 2009, Ricardo Martinelli, an American-educated businessperson who owns a chain of supermarkets in Panama, became president. He won the election by a landslide, gaining more than 60 percent of the votes. Martinelli has worked to eliminate corruption and to help the poor, especially through tax reform. He has also worked to improve Panama's infrastructure—its roads, bridges, electrical system, and docks—so that it can grow as a vital hub of global shipping.

The president appoints the members of the cabinet, who are called ministers. They advise the president on specific areas such areas as health, foreign relations, and education.

The Legislature

The law-making body in Panama is called the National Assembly. It is unicameral, meaning it has only one house (the United States is bicameral, having two houses). The National Assembly has seventy-one deputies who are elected for five-year terms.

The National Assembly meets in a modern building in Panama City.

A Visit to Panama City

Located on the Pacific end of the Panama Canal, the capital city had a population of 880,691 in 2010. About one-third of the people in Panama live in the city and its suburbs. The city has become like many international cities, boasting a skyline filled with great skyscrapers.

Founded almost five hundred years ago by Pedro Arias de Ávila, the city was plundered and destroyed by the pirate Henry Morgan and his men in 1671. Some remains of the original city, called Panamá Viejo (Old Panama), can still be seen. Today, ancient walls of the cathedral and other buildings still stand.

Panama City was rebuilt enclosed in a wall for protection. This section of the city is now called Casco Viejo, or the Old Quarter (below). This older part of the city features many churches, theaters, and other historic buildings, including the beautiful white presidential palace called Palace of the Herons, which was built in 1673.

Towering skyscrapers dominate the newer parts of the city. Latin America's second-tallest building is the city's seventy-story Trump Ocean Club, a hotel and condominium tower. Most of the growth has occurred since the canal was turned over to Panama. The city also has a new subway system that everyone hopes will help relieve some of the dense traffic that jams the streets.

Panama City

The way deputies are elected depends on where they are from. Members from rural districts are elected if they receive the most votes. In urban areas, seats are allotted on the basis of the proportion of the population that votes for a particular political party. For example, if a party wins 25 percent of the vote, one-fourth of the seats in the National Assembly are allotted to that party.

The Court System

The judicial branch of government is headed by the Supreme Court of Justice. Nine judges, or justices, are appointed for ten-year terms.

The Supreme Court appoints the justices for the superior district courts, which are courts of appeal that review lower court

National Government of Panama

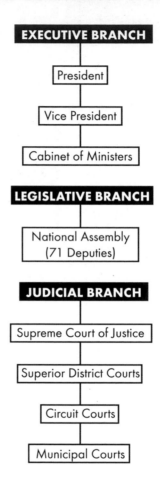

EXECUTIVE BRANCH

President

Vice President

Cabinet of Ministers

LEGISLATIVE BRANCH

National Assembly
(71 Deputies)

JUDICIAL BRANCH

Supreme Court of Justice

Superior District Courts

Circuit Courts

Municipal Courts

decisions. The judges on the superior district courts appoint the judges to the circuit courts and municipal courts, where trials are held. A separate system of courts, called the Electoral Tribunal, is responsible for ensuring the legality of elections.

In 2014, Panama instituted a new legal system in which an investigation must take place before a person can be charged with a crime. Once charged, a person can usually get out of jail while awaiting trial. In the old system, an accused person could wait in jail for several years while the crime was investigated and the trial was held.

General Manuel Noriega ruled Panama for six years.

The Military

Dictators who came from the military ruled Panama from 1968 to 1989, when the United States invaded Panama and overthrew General Manuel Noriega. In 1994, Panama ratified (approved) a constitutional amendment prohibiting the creation of a regular army. Today, Panama has only a small national security force called the Panamanian Public Security Forces. It includes the national police, a maritime service similar to the Coast Guard, and an investigating police force. The constitution has since been changed to allow a temporary special military to be formed, but only if Panama is attacked by forces outside the country.

Provinces and Comarcas

From the time modern Panama was formed in 1903, it has been divided into regions called provinces. The provinces of Panama are: Bocas del Toro, Chiriquí, Veraguas, Coclé, Herrera, Los Santos, Colón, Panama, and Darién. The provinces are divided into districts, which are divided into *corregimientos*, or municipalities.

In addition to the provinces, Panama has regions called *comarcas indígenas*, or just *comarcas*. They are the territories—sometimes called reservations—occupied and governed

In Darién, many houses are built on stilts to protect them from flooding.

by indigenous people. The Emberá-Wounaan Comarca is divided into two parts within Darién. By far the largest comarca is the Ngöbe-Buglé Comarca in the west, between Chiriquí and Veraguas. The Guna Yala Comarca consists of the Guna Yala, or San Blas, Islands and the strip of coastal land adjacent to the islands. The Guna people have two smaller comarcas that are part of Panama Province and Darién Province.

The comarcas are run by their own governments, usually a tribal council or general congress. A chosen leader is called a *cacique*. The comarcas also

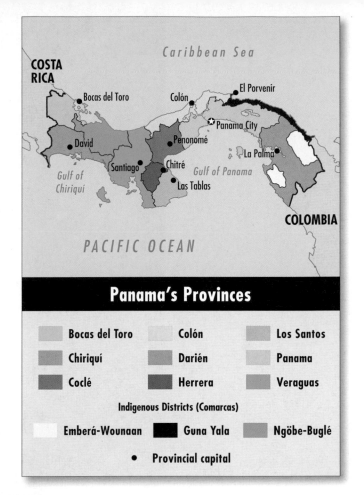

Panama's Provinces

Bocas del Toro	Colón	Los Santos
Chiriquí	Darién	Panama
Coclé	Herrera	Veraguas

Indigenous Districts (Comarcas)

Emberá-Wounaan	Guna Yala	Ngöbe-Buglé

● Provincial capital

Red, White, and Blue

The Panamanian flag was first used in 1904 and was officially adopted in 1925. It was designed by the family of Manuel Amador Guerrero, the first president of Panama.

The flag consists of four rectangles: two white, one red, and one blue. One of the white rectangles contains a blue star and the other a red star. The white of the flag represents peace. The blue stands for purity and honesty, and the red for the authority and law of the country.

The leader of an Emberá village near Lake Bayano

send representatives to the National Assembly. However, many of the indigenous leaders think that the national government and businesses do not listen to their own decisions and opinions.

Although they are quite different in many ways, the indigenous tribes have joined together to preserve their interests. They work together in the National Coordinating Body of Indigenous Peoples in Panama (COONAPIP), an organization that is fighting to preserve their rights to their land.

The National Anthem

"Himno Istmeño" ("Hymn of the Isthmus"), the national anthem of Panama, was first adopted in 1906 and confirmed in 1925. The words are by Jerónimo de la Ossa, and the music is by Santos Jorge.

Spanish lyrics

Alcanzamos por fin la victoria
En el campo feliz de la unión;
Con ardientes fulgores de gloria
Se ilumina la nueva nación.
Con ardientes fulgores de gloria
Se ilumina la nueva nación.

Es preciso cubrir con un velo
Del pasado el calvario y la cruz;
Y que adorne el azul de tu cielo
De concordia la espléndida luz.

El progreso acaricia tus lares.
Al compás de sublime canción,
Ves rugir a tus pies ambos mares
Que dan rumbo a tu noble misión.

Alcanzamos por fin la victoria
En el campo feliz de la unión;
Con ardientes fulgores de gloria
Se ilumina la nueva nación.
Con ardientes fulgores de gloria
Se ilumina la nueva nación.

English translation

At last we reached victory
In the joyous field of the union;
With ardent fires of glory
A new nation is alight.
With ardent fires of glory
A new nation is alight.

It is necessary to cover with a veil
The past times of Calvary and cross;
Let now the blue skies be adorned with
The splendid light of the concord.

Progress caresses your path.
To the rhythm of a sublime song,
You see both your seas roar at your feet
Giving you a path to your noble mission.

At last we reached victory
In the joyous field of the union;
With ardent fires of glory
A new nation is alight.
With ardent fires of glory
A new nation is alight.

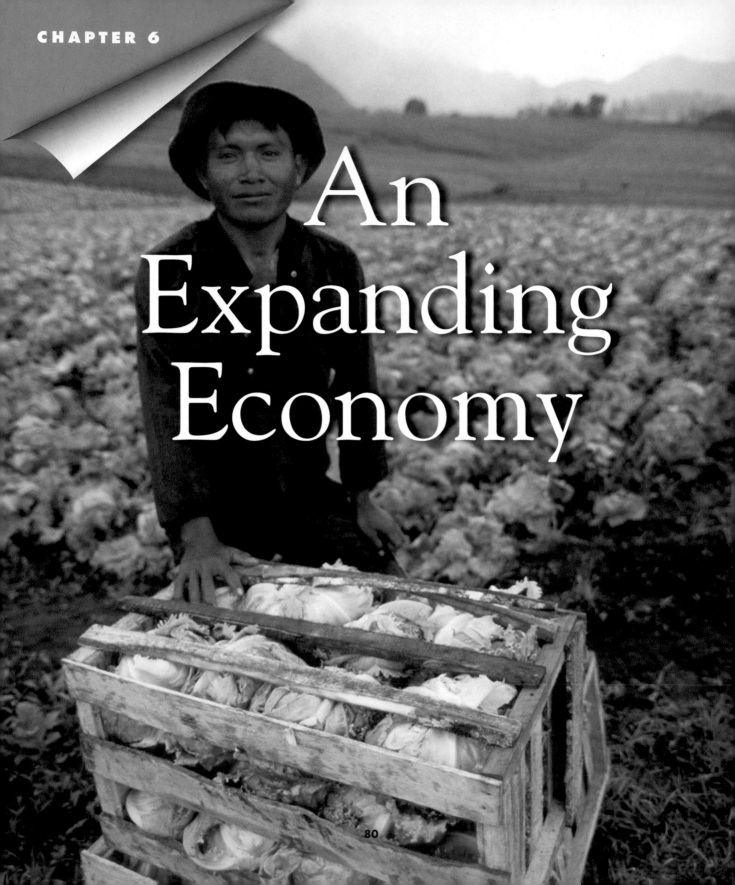

CHAPTER 6

An Expanding Economy

PANAMA IS THE LEADER AMONG ALL LATIN AMERICAN countries in terms of economic growth after many years of being near the bottom. In 2012, Panama's economy grew by almost 11 percent. Many Panamanians are now enjoying their thriving economy. However, not all Panamanians feel as if they're succeeding. A full 17 percent of the labor force still works in agriculture, which makes up only 3.8 percent of the economy. The presence of the canal makes the portion of the economy based on services very high—almost 80 percent in 2012. Industry is second, at 16.8 percent. Unemployment in 2012 was very low—less than 5 percent of workers in Panama were without jobs.

Agriculture

For many years the main economic activity for Panamanians was farming. Most of the farms were subsistence farms, which means that they were only large enough to support the family

Opposite: **Lettuce is one of the many vegetables grown in Panama. Most vegetable farms are in the mountainous regions of western Panama.**

Banana Power

Bananas have been cultivated for at least seven thousand years. They are the world's largest flowering plant. Although they are called banana trees, banana plants are like garden flowers—they grow quickly, produce one bunch of bananas from the reddish flower, and then die back. Shoots on the base of the stem develop into the next year's growth.

Bananas require a fairly steady temperature that doesn't fall below 52 degrees Fahrenheit (11 degrees Celsius). There can't be much wind because bananas have shallow roots that can easily be pulled out of the ground. Rain needs to fall throughout the year and total at least 70 inches (178 cm). Bocas del Toro and Chiriquí provinces in the west fit these requirements.

In the 1950s, a disease called the Panama disease killed banana plants throughout Central America. This disease is a fungus that eats the roots of the plants. Farmers began growing a type of banana that was resistant to the disease, but this fruit wasn't quite as tasty. In the 1990s, a more vicious strain of Panama disease hit, and once again bananas were in danger. Scientists are working to develop a banana that resists the new fungus.

who worked the land. There was nothing left over to sell to obtain cash. Much of Panama's productive land is now planted with bananas to be exported to other countries. Other export crops include rice, sugarcane, cocoa beans, coffee, and coconuts.

Panama's forests are an important source of hardwoods, especially mahogany. This beautiful reddish wood is used for expensive furniture. The hard, durable, dark wood called teak is being planted in areas that have been deforested. It is used in outdoor items such as boats and patio furniture.

Manufacturing and Mining

Manufacturing did not become an important part of the Panamanian economy until the middle of the twentieth century. Today, the largest industries are food processing and oil refining. Shoes, clothing, paper, chemicals, and cement are also produced in Panama.

Gold has been mined in Panama for centuries, and small amounts of it continue to be removed from the ground. Panama's copper deposits are among the largest on earth. But companies have been slow in developing the copper mining industry. This is in part because of the high cost of getting to the metal. Also, indigenous people have often joined with environmentalists to slow the mining of copper in the

A worker in Panama roasts coffee beans. This process increases the flavor of the beans.

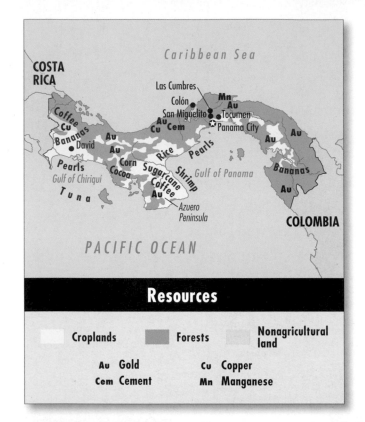

Caribbean Sea

COSTA RICA

Las Cumbres
Colón
San Miguelito
David
Tocumen
Panama City
COLOMBIA

Coffee
Cu
Bananas
Au
Au
Cu
Cem
Mn
Au
Au
Cem
Au
Pearls
Corn
Cocoa
Rice
Pearls
Gulf of Panama
Bananas
Au
Pearls
Gulf of Chiriquí
Sugarcane
Coffee
Au
Shrimp
Tuna
Azuero
Peninsula

PACIFIC OCEAN

Resources

| | Croplands | | Forests | | Nonagricultural land |

Au **Gold**   Cu **Copper**
Cem **Cement**   Mn **Manganese**

rain forests. A Canadian company is building a huge open-pit copper mine in the rain forest on the Atlantic coast. Scheduled to open in 2016 or 2017, it is the biggest project in Panama since the canal was built.

The Ngöbe-Buglé people were able to get the government to pass a law prohibiting mining in their comarca. This law, signed in 2012, cancelled all mining agreements that were signed in the past.

Workers at a gold mine in Colón

What Panama Grows, Makes, and Mines

AGRICULTURE (2010)

Sugarcane	2,095,010 metric tons
Bananas	338,280 metric tons
Rice	274,020 metric tons

MANUFACTURING (VALUE ADDED, 2006)

Food products	US$468,000,000
Beverages	US$167,000,000
Cement, bricks, ceramics	US$82,000,000

MINING (2009)

Limestone	270,000 metric tons
Gold	800 kilograms

Trade

The most important port on the Caribbean coast is Cristóbal. On the Pacific coast the main port is at Balboa. Colón has the second-largest free trade zone in the world. That means materials can be brought into its port, products can be manufactured from those materials, and those products can be shipped out again, all without taxes.

Almost one-fourth of all goods imported into Panama come from the United States. These goods include such items as cell phones, fuel products, and medications. Transportation equipment and chemicals are also imported. Panama imports goods from Mexico, Japan, and Ecuador as well.

Panama's major exports include food products such as

Passengers enjoy a good view as a cruise ship moves through the Miraflores Locks on the Panama Canal.

bananas, shrimp, and coffee. Many Panamanian goods are shipped to the United States, Canada, and Costa Rica.

In 2007, Panama and the United States signed a free trade agreement that went into effect in 2012. Under this agreement, companies no longer have to pay taxes on most goods traded between the two countries. This will likely increase trade between Panama and the United States.

The Canal

Service industries play a huge part in Panama's economy, in large part because of the canal. In 2013, the fee for a big containership to go through the Panama Canal rose to $450,000 for a ship carrying 4,500 containers. A container is a huge steel box that can be moved directly from a ship onto a truck or train. Cruise ships pay $134 per bed on the ship. For a small yacht—one less than 50 feet (15 m) long—it costs about $800 to transit the canal. Those fees belong to Panama.

The size of ships is often referred to as Panamax, meaning they are as big as they can be and still go through the Panama Canal. The size is determined by the length and width of the chambers in the locks, as well as by the height of the Bridge of the Americas. That bridge, finished in 1962, is located at the Pacific entrance to the canal. It has a clearance of 201 feet (61 m) at high tide.

Ship size that is bigger than Panamax is called post-Panamax. About half of all containerships (the preferred way of shipping) are post-Panamax ships. That number will only grow. For this reason, it is even more important to Panama that the canal be expanded.

Bridges in Panama City

From the beginning, bridges were planned as part of the canal. Without them, Panamanians on the east side of the canal could not easily reach the west side. But no bridges were built right away. Instead, ferries were used to move cars and people between the two sections of Panama. Not until 1955 did the United States commit to building a permanent bridge.

At the Pacific end of the canal is the beautiful Bridge of the Americas, built in the early 1960s. It carries four lanes of traffic. By the start of the twenty-first century, more than thirty-five thousand cars a day were traveling the Bridge of the Americas. It had become a bottleneck to the flow of traffic. The Centennial Bridge (left), located 9.3 miles (15 km) north of the first bridge, opened in 2004. This gave drivers some relief because both bridges were being used.

The Canal by the Numbers

	Old Canal	Expansion
Lock chamber width	110 feet (33.5 m)	180 feet (55 m)
Lock chamber length	1,050 feet (320 m)	1,400 feet (427 m)
Draft (depth below water)	40 feet (12 m)	60 feet (18 m)
Highest capacity of ship	52,000 tons	119,000 tons

Each lock gate is 7 feet (2.1 m) thick and weighs 700 tons
The canal is 48 miles (77 km) long

The expansion of the Panama Canal began in 2007 and is expected to take almost a decade to complete.

Some experts think that the expansion of the canal won't be beneficial for very long. Already, shipbuilders are building ships bigger than the expanded canal can handle. There is also going to be competition from other routes that ships can take.

By the year 2030, the Arctic Ocean may be free of ice for nine months of the year. If so, ships will need the Panama Canal only a quarter of the year. That will be devastating for Panamanians.

Other Services

Tourism has become a major industry in Panama. In 2012, more than two million visitors arrived in the nation. The tourists provide work for waiters and hoteliers, taxi drivers and tour guides. It is estimated that nearly 10 percent of the total income of the country comes from tourism.

Panama has also turned itself into a major banking center. There are close to eighty banks in Panama, many of them branches of big banks in other countries.

Another less common service in Panama is ship registry. Every ship has to be registered, but it doesn't have to be reg-

Dozens of dams have been built in Panama to provide electricity to the nation.

istered in the home country of its owner or where it is used. Instead, ships can be registered in whatever country the ship's owner chooses. An owner may pick a specific country because registration is cheaper there or it saves money in taxes. Because Panama charges less than most countries for ships to be registered, more than 20 percent of the world's ships are registered there. As a result, on the whole, Panama makes a great deal of money with its ship registry.

Powering the Growth

Panama tries to meet most of its electrical needs by building hydroelectric dams across rivers. The power of the moving water turns turbines that generate electricity, providing more than half the nation's power.

The first hydroelectric dam in Panama was built on the Bayano River in Darién Province in 1976. The lake created, called Bayano Lake, flooded more than 135 square miles (350 sq km) of rain forest. It forced more than two thousand Guna people and five hundred Emberá people out of their homes. It also destroyed the habitat of many water-dwelling species of plants and animals.

Fortuna Dam in western Panama produces more electricity—30 percent of the country's needs—than any other dam in the country. When it was built in 1984, the dam was 197 feet (60 m) tall, but it was made half again as high by 1994. That provided a lot more power.

Money Facts

Panama uses the American dollar for its paper currency, but the nation has its own coins. The coins are called balboas in honor of Vasco Núñez de Balboa, who crossed Panama and became the first European to see the Pacific Ocean in the Western Hemisphere. Each balboa is broken into 100 centesimos, or cents. Coins have values of 1 centesimo, 5 centesimos, and 1/10, 1/4, and 1/2 balboa, which correspond to the American penny, nickel, dime, quarter, and half-dollar. Some 1 centesimo coins show an indigenous hero named Urracá. He was a Guaymí leader who fought against the Spanish conquerors in the 1520s.

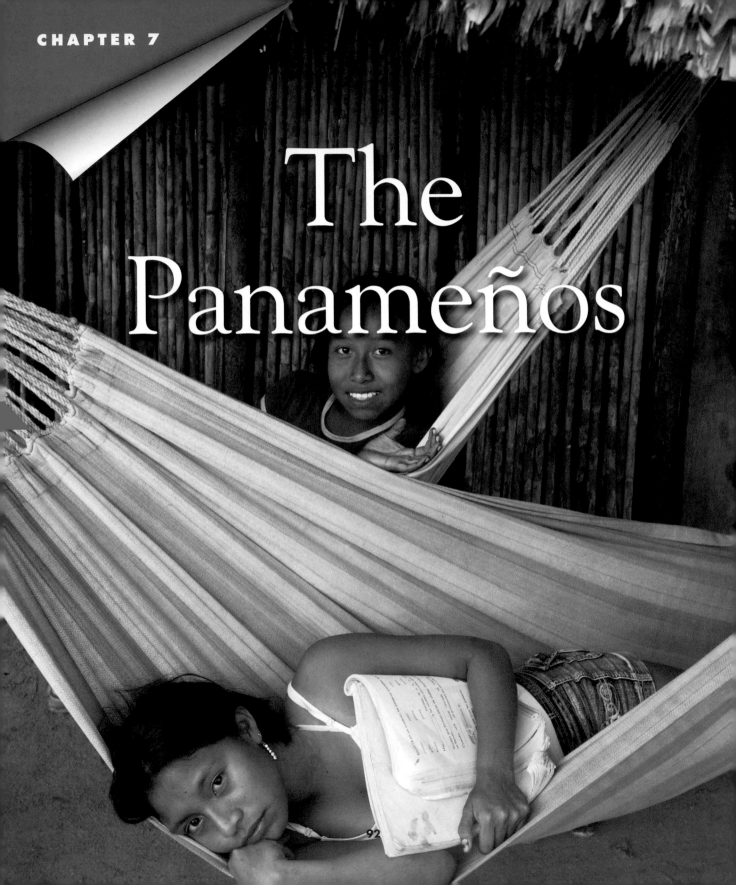

CHAPTER 7

The Panameños

ABOUT 3.5 MILLION PEOPLE LIVE IN PANAMA. That's about the number of people who live in the state of Connecticut. They call themselves *Panameños*. More than half of the people in Panama live in or near Panama City and Colón, the cities that lie at either end of the canal. After the Canal Zone ceased to exist, many fishing villages that lay just outside the cities were swallowed up as the cities quickly expanded.

Opposite: **Teenagers relax in hammocks in the San Blas Islands. Nearly half the people in Panama are less than twenty-five years old.**

Ethnic Groups

In the past five centuries, many different people have come to Panama from many different parts of the world. As a result, today's Panamanians are a mix of many different ethnic groups. The largest group in Panama today is the mestizos. *Mestizo* is a Spanish word for a person whose ethnic heritage is a combination of European and Indian. In Panama, a mestizo may also have some Chinese or African ancestors.

Population of Major Cities (2010 est.)	
Panama City	880,691
San Miguelito	315,019
Tocumen	103,117
David	89,442
Las Cumbres	89,000
Colón	78,000

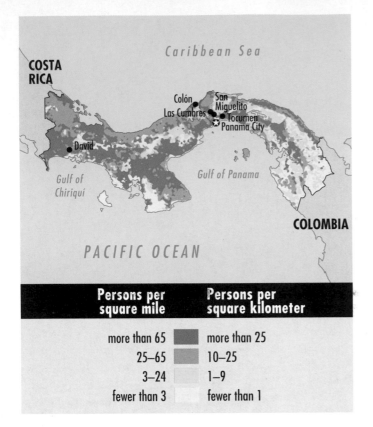

Persons per square mile	Persons per square kilometer
more than 65	more than 25
25–65	10–25
3–24	1–9
fewer than 3	fewer than 1

Black Panamanians are sometimes called Afro-Panamanians. Some black Panamanians are descended from enslaved Africans who were brought to Panama. Others are descended from people of the Caribbean Islands who came to Panama to work on the canal. At the time the canal was being built, Colón was an important, growing city. Many immigrants from the West Indies arrived and were welcome because they spoke English. Even so, they were paid less than white workers doing the same jobs. Today, most of the people in Colón are descended from Indians and Africans.

Panama has had a sizable Chinese population since Americans brought in Chinese workers to help build the Panama Railroad in the 1850s. Although they were not always granted full rights, since 1946, all Chinese born in Panama have been considered Panamanian citizens. Today, Chinese Panamanians number about 150,000, making them the largest Chinese community in Central America.

Society

The elite people in Panama are mostly descended from the Spaniards who settled the isthmus. Most high government officials come from this group.

Ethnic Groups (2010 census)

Mestizo	65%
Black, or black and Indian	16%
Indian	12%
White	7%

Middle-class Panamanians make up a much larger group. They mostly live in Panama City, where they own their own homes or live in nice apartments. They are usually of European descent or mestizo. Some middle-class people have moved up into the elite class by becoming doctors or other highly educated professionals.

The working classes are mostly mestizo or black. Few own land or their own homes. They work at whatever jobs they can find, often as laborers and household help. Outside the city, they are primarily subsistence farmers or farm laborers.

A woman lights candles during a Chinese lunar new year celebration in Panama City.

Indigenous Peoples

When the Spanish came to Panama in the sixteenth century, there were probably several hundred thousand Indians living there. Their numbers shrank, though, as they died from European diseases or were killed. Today, the descendants of the people who originally lived along the isthmus make up about 12 percent of Panama's population.

The government has combined five indigenous groups into three for official recognition because their cultures are similar. The groups that have their own comarcas, or territories, are called Guna; Guaymí (also called Ngöbe-Buglé); and Emberá-Wounaan.

An indigenous village in Panama in the early 1500s

In recent years, Guna people have started writing down stories in their own language. They have also been writing histories taken from their oral traditions. In 2004, the Guna leaders began working to create a standard way of writing their language, which is very different from Spanish. Here is an example given by Kayla Price, Director of Language Acquisition Center at the University of Houston in Texas:

English: If I say that I want to write in my language, in order to better understand my past, I am going to write . . .

Guna: *An sogdibe an an gaya narmakbie, an igar danikid wisguegala, an garda narmaknaidi . . .*

The Guna

The first indigenous people to be recognized by the Panamanian government were the Guna people of the San Blas Islands. They call their home Guna Yala. The archipelago includes more than 360 islands, which are home to about forty thousand Guna people. The Guna are concerned about climate change because the warming of our planet is raising the level of the ocean. Most islands are so low-lying that they will be flooded.

Because Guna Yala is autonomous, or self-governing, a visitor needs to have a passport to cross from Panama to the islands. Guna Yala has its own flag, which is red, yellow, and green. Individual Guna people cannot leave their islands without permission from the chief. Nor can outsiders come in and set up businesses.

Guna women commonly decorate their faces with paint.

The Guna people protect the coral reefs near their outer islands. They do not permit scuba diving along the reefs, though they do allow snorkeling. Visitors who want to visit many islands must pay a fee for every island they want to explore.

Guna women are known for their beautiful and colorful needlework called *molas*. These are panels of intricate embroidery that are worn as the front and back of the women's blouses. Molas probably originated from the body painting the Guna people have done throughout history.

The Ngöbe-Buglé

The Ngöbe (also called Guaymí) and the Buglé people together make up the largest indigenous group, with a population of about 110,000. They live in the western part of Panama, mainly in Chiriquí Province. In 1997, a large number of Ngöbe-Buglé people marched to Panama City to demand ownership of their land. They were ultimately granted their own comarca.

In 2012, Ngöbe-Buglé activists blocked the single main road for several days. The action was to protest mining and hydroelectric projects that would have harmed their comarca.

A Ngöbe boy shoots a slingshot.

They were successful—from now on any project must get the people's approval in advance.

The Emberá-Wounaan

The Emberá and Wounaan are sometimes called Chocós because they once lived in the Chocó province of Colombia. These two groups are linked together because they share much of the same geographic area and have cultural similarities. This combined group's comarca was created in 1983.

Ngöbe-Buglé people carrying the flag of their comarca protest changes to mining laws, which would allow companies to mine in indigenous areas.

Both groups are known for their amazing coiled baskets woven by the women. The Emberá and the Wounaan were mainly hunter-gatherers until recent decades. Now they grow bananas and plantains as commercial crops, which the whole community owns together. Once, each village had a chieftain, but now the people form committees to make decisions. Their forests are very important to them, and they try to keep outsiders from logging the land illegally. An Emberá Indian told a reporter, "The forest is our mother. But it is still beautiful, it is ours and we have to look after it because without it we are nothing."

Baskets woven by the Emberá people are renowned for their bold designs.

Other Indigenous Peoples

Other groups without official recognition include the Naso, or Teribe, who live in the mountainous forests of Bocas del Toro in the west. Unlike most indigenous peoples, the Naso still have a king or queen, though he or she is now elected from among the royal family. Although they also speak Spanish, the Naso use their own language, Teribe, at least among themselves. Most are subsistence farmers or fishers who also speak Spanish.

The government has recently recognized another language, that of the Bribri. It is primarily a language of Costa Rica but is also spoken in western Panama. Only a few thousand Bribri-speaking people live in the Talamanca Mountains.

Naso men fish in a traditional dugout boat.

Indigenous Life

Most indigenous Panamanians live far from the cities. They blend tradition with elements of modern Panamanian society, working together to maintain their own cultures as they decide how to react to pressures from outside their community.

Many indigenous people wear small cloths called loincloths suspended from their waists when they are in their own home. They change into western-style clothes when they interact with outsiders. The women tend to wear lots of beaded, silver, and gold jewelry.

A sign in Panama City warns drivers that a road is a dead end.

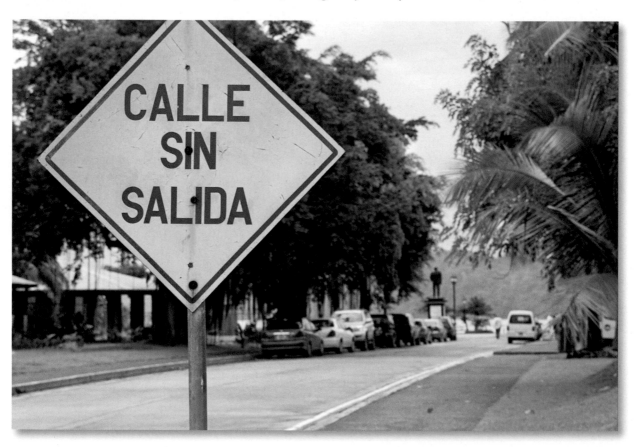

Some Spanish Words and Phrases

Por favor	Please
Gracias	Thank you
De nada	You're welcome
Sí	Yes
¡Hola!	Hello
¿Habla inglés?	Do you speak English?
No hablo español	I don't speak Spanish

Indigenous houses are often raised high on stilts. These houses might be 10 feet (3 m) above the ground, with stairs going up into them from below. The raised houses protect the people from wild animals, as well as from flooding in the rainy season.

Some indigenous people still hunt with darts and arrows that have a poisonous substance on the tips. They fish in the rivers by standing in a dugout canoe and spearing the fish they see in the water below. Most river people use dugout canoes that are carved or burned from a single tree trunk. Dugouts can be quite small, for use by children learning to fish, or large enough to hold an entire village.

Speaking Spanish

Spanish is the official language of Panama. Panamanians have their own way of speaking the language. Unlike most Spanish-speakers, Panamanians drop the *s* sound at the end of a word. For example, the word *vamos*, which means "Let's go," is pronounced VAH-moh by Panamanians, instead of VAH-mohs. Because of Panama's long association with the United States, Panamanians also use many English words.

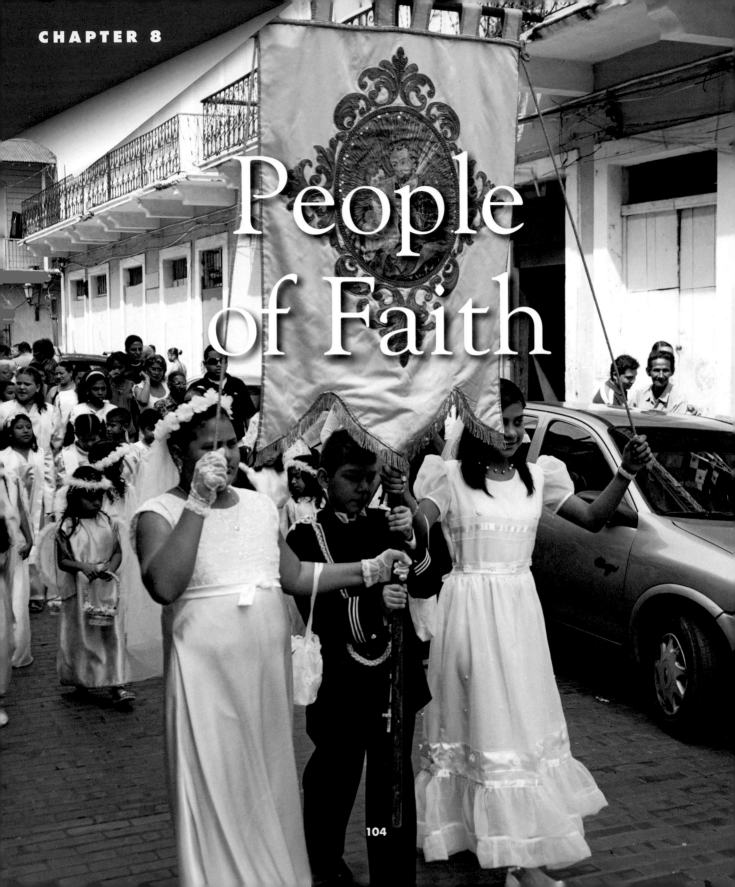

CHAPTER 8

People of Faith

THE PANAMANIAN CONSTITUTION ENSURES FREEDOM of religion. The government does not collect statistics on religion, but experts estimate that about 84 percent of the people are Roman Catholic. Most other Panamanians are Protestant. There are also small numbers of Baha'is, Muslims, and Jews.

Roman Catholicism

Today, Panama is primarily a Catholic country. Although there is no official religion, Catholicism is given some preference. For example, public schools teach about Catholicism, although parents can ask that their children not be taught religion.

The nation's main cathedral, in Panama City, is the Metropolitan Cathedral of Santa María la Antigua. Construction on it began in 1688 and took more than a hundred years to complete.

The major religious holidays in Panama are Christmas and Easter. Panama City is famed for its Christmas parade. Bands of drummers, other musicians, and dancers accompany color-

Religion in Panama

Roman Catholic	84%
Evangelical Christian	10%
Other Protestant	4%
Other	2%

The Church and a Saint

The Church of San Pedro, built in 1550 on Taboga Island in the Gulf of Panama, is the oldest existing church in Panama, and the second oldest in the Western Hemisphere. The island was the first port Europeans built on the Pacific coast. This "island of flowers," as it is known, can be reached by ferry from Panama City. Some people have claimed that Rose of Lima, who in 1671 became the first Catholic saint from the Americas, was born on Taboga Island in 1586. Her official biography, however, says she was born in Lima, Peru.

ful floats down the main streets. Many people attend a mass at church on Christmas Eve, and then at midnight the cracks of fireworks echo through the air.

Panama City also has a famed celebration of Carnival, the four days before the start of Lent, a quiet and somber period leading up to Easter. Carnival is filled with masks, music, and dance, and celebrations that go on night and day. In the few days before Easter, religious processions wind through the streets.

Other Religions

About 14 percent of Panamanians belong to various Protestant denominations. The largest is Assembly of God, with more than eight hundred congregations throughout the country. It and several other denominations are called evangelical, meaning they accept the Bible as the final authority for belief.

Baha'i is a faith that incorporates all religions and emphasizes the unity of all people. It was founded about 150 years ago in Iran. Although the Baha'i faith has spread throughout the world, it has only seven major houses of worship. One of them is in Panama, on a high hill in Panama City. The Baha'i faith has been in Panama since the 1940s and is practiced by less than 2 percent of the people. Baha'i is very popular among the Ngöbe.

Less than 1 percent of Panamanians are Muslims, people who follow the religion Islam. Islam first came to Panama with some African slaves in the 1550s. However, all traces of those early Muslims disappeared. In the nineteenth century, other immigrants who practiced Islam came to work on the railroad or the canal. An estimated twenty-four thousand Muslims live in the country, most in Panama City or Colón. An Islamic cultural center was built in Colón in 1982. There are now

During Carnival, people dress in elaborate costumes for parades through the streets.

two mosques (Muslim houses of worship) in Panama City, and several others elsewhere.

About eight thousand Jews live in Panama, most in Panama City, especially in the former Canal Zone. Some Jews also live in Colón and David. The largest synagogue, or Jewish house of worship, is the orthodox Shevet Achim in Panama City.

Indigenous Faiths

All Baha'i temples have nine sides and are topped by a dome. Inside, people meet in a single large room that has no statues or pictures.

People outside the indigenous communities have a difficult time finding out about the traditional religious beliefs of the native peoples. Their faith is handed down by oral tradition through stories told by the elders—a ritual learned purely

by seeing it carried out. Nothing is written down. In most Panamanian indigenous religions, there is a spiritual leader called a shaman who is in touch with the spirit in all things, both good and bad. Shamans are often healers who know which plants are useful in treating various illnesses.

When the Spanish conquistadores traveled to Panama in the 1500s, they were looking for gold, but they were also determined to convert the indigenous people to Christianity. The conquistadores were not completely successful in Panama. Many Panamanian Indians today mix Christianity with elements from their traditional religions, such as dancing and body painting.

In Wounaan and Emberá cultures, people paint their bodies for religious ceremonies using the black juice of a jagua fruit. Unlike tattoos, these designs are not permanent. Some Indian villages are now attracting tourists who want to observe the body painting and the dancing.

The body paint used by the Emberá and Wounaan people lasts between one and two weeks.

CHAPTER 9

The Panamanian Way

MUSIC AND DANCE ARE IMPORTANT PARTS OF life in Panama. Panama's culture of music comes from as many ethnic groups as have made their homes there, starting with the indigenous people. People who later came to Panama brought music from their homes in Africa and the Caribbean islands.

Young people today dance to salsa, reggae, merengue, and other types of music. Reggae is a rhythmic music that started in Jamaica in the 1960s. Panamanians adapted it into their own style of music for dancing, called *reggae en Español*, meaning "Spanish reggae."

Panamanian Music

Several instruments are particularly important to Panamanian music. These include the *mejoranera*, a type of guitar with five strings. A mejoranera is typically used to accompany a romantic ballad called a *mejorana*.

Opposite: **A Guna man plays a traditional flute made from bamboo reeds.**

The *guiro* and conga drums add rhythm to modern folk dance. The guiro is a dried gourd that has had grooves cut into the side. The musician runs a rod across the grooves in the guiro, creating a distinctive sound. These instruments are used in contemporary music called *típico*.

The traditional dance of Panama is called the *tamborito*, which means "little drum." This dance is usually performed by couples to the accompaniment of drums and a chorus of women. People stomp their feet, adding to the sounds.

Conga drums provide the rhythm for much Panamanian folk music.

Panamanians love movies, and for the most part have been content with watching the big films from the United States. Since 2012, however, Panama City has hosted an annual international film festival.

Arts

One of Panama's first major artists was Roberto Lewis. After training in Paris, France, he returned to Panama in 1907 to install murals he had painted on the walls of the new National Theater building. Today, these masterpieces are among the prides of Panama City.

Another important Panamanian artist is Chafil Cheucarama, a Wounaan from Darién. He has won prizes for his illustrations

Women's national dresses, called polleras, are often decorated with flower designs.

of children's books and is known for his small, delicate sculptures.

Like Cheucarama, many Panamanian sculptors work with the wood that grows in their own country. Cocobolo wood is a beautiful dark red wood that is sometimes used for chess pieces. Much softer is the plant material called tagua, or vegetable ivory. The nuts harden into an ivory-like material when exposed to air and can be carved in beautiful little pieces.

One of the most remarkable arts in Panama is *mola*, or blouse panel, made by the Guna people. It is a colorful, complex type of embroidery. Originally used for women's dresses, it is now used to make wall hangings.

Likewise, the women's dresses called *polleras*, made throughout Panama and Central America, are works of wearable art. Women wear this national dress for many special occasions. It developed out of the women's dresses of the sixteenth century. This dress is usually white, made in several full ruffles with fancy embroidery on it.

An Assortment of Sports

Panamanians are wild about sports. They love soccer and basketball, but the most popular sport is probably baseball. Children start playing baseball very young, sometimes as early as four years of age. U.S. Major League Baseball player and coach Rod Carew is from Panama. His family immigrated to the United States when he was fourteen. Retired New York Yankees pitcher Mariano Rivera is a native of La Chorrera. With his wicked fastball, Rivera is regarded as a good bet to be elected to the Baseball Hall of Fame. Catcher Carlos Ruiz of the Philadelphia Phillies is from David. He caught a perfect game in 2010 and has played in a World Series.

Rod Carew was one of the most consistent hitters in Major League Baseball. He was elected to the National Baseball Hall of Fame in 1981.

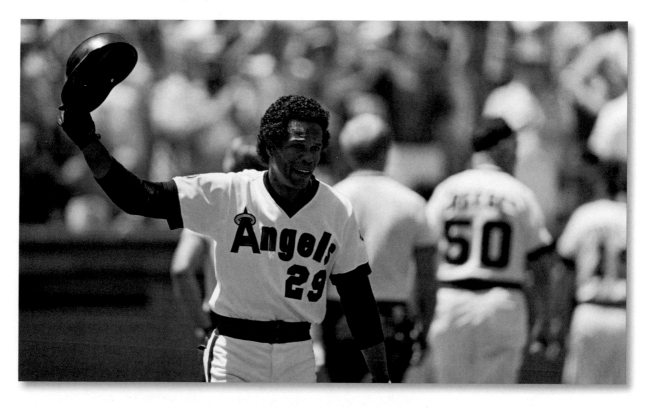

Boxing champ Alfonso Teofilo Brown, usually called Panama Al Brown, was a native of Colón. Brown became interested in boxing when he first saw American soldiers boxing in the Canal Zone. Once he started the sport, Brown turned professional very quickly, because his long arms and great height gave him an important advantage over other bantamweight and featherweight boxers. He became the first Hispanic world boxing champion in 1929. Roberto Durán, a native of Guararé, is regarded by many as one of the greatest lightweight boxers of all time.

Panamanian jockey Laffit Pincay Jr. retired in 2003 with the most thoroughbred racing victories in history at that time. He won 9,530 races in a career that lasted more than thirty-five years.

In 1984, Laffit Pincay Jr. (in yellow) rode a horse named Swale to victory at the Kentucky Derby, the most prestigious horse race in the United States.

The Caribbean side of Panama is known for its great surfing, especially from November to April. During the remainder of the year the sea is too calm to surf. Panama is famous for waves called barrels, which break in the middle, leaving a large hole in which the surfer rides. Surfing is best on the Pacific coast in April, May, and June.

Surfers ride a horse to the sea on Wizard Beach, a top surfing spot in the Bocas del Toro islands.

Panama in the Olympics

Lloyd La Beach was the first Panamanian to win an Olympic medal. A sprinter, he won two bronze medals in the 1948 Olympics. Since then, the nation has won only one more medal, but it was gold. It went to Irving Saladino (left) for the men's long jump at the 2008 Olympics. It was also the first Olympic gold medal ever won by a man from a Central American country. (A Costa Rican woman, Claudia Poll, won a gold medal in swimming in the 1988 Games.)

The Panamanian Way   **117**

CHAPTER 10

Panamanian Life

IN THE PAST, THE DAILY LIFE OF PANAMANIANS depended greatly on where they lived. If they lived in the Canal Zone, their lives were more privileged. But today, the Canal Zone has disappeared. Increasing wealth is bringing good things to more people. People who live in rural areas, however, still tend to be poorer than those who live in the cities near the canal.

Opposite: **Panamanian children leave school for the day. About 15 percent of the government budget is devoted to education.**

Schooltime

In Panama, children are required to attend six years of primary school and three years of middle school. Many children then continue on to high school. The school year runs from April to December. The school day usually starts between 8:00 and 9:00 a.m. and runs until 2:00 or 3:00 p.m. The literacy rate has risen steadily in the last hundred years. About 94 percent of Panamanians can now read and write.

Students in Panama City head into a building at the Technological University of Panama, the nation's second-largest university. The school has a highly respected engineering program.

There are fourteen colleges and universities in Panama. The largest is the University of Panama, which has campuses all over the country, but the main campus is in Panama City. More than sixty thousand students attend the University of Panama.

Panama has a high crime rate, especially in Panama City and Colón, where street gangs flourish. To protect young people, the Panamanian government has put in place a strict curfew for people under the age of eighteen. Young people have to be home by 8:00 p.m. on Sundays through Thursdays, and 11:00 p.m. on Fridays and Saturdays, unless they are accompanied by an adult. They can also be out if they attend night classes or have a job, but in those cases they need to carry special identification. If young people are out on their own past curfew, they are taken to a police station until their legal adult guardian comes to get them.

National Holidays

New Year's Day	January 1
Martyrs' Day	January 9
Carnival Day	February or March
Good Friday	March or April
Labor Day	May 1
Independence from Colombia Day	November 3
Colón Day	November 5
First Cry for Independence Day	November 10
Independence from Spain Day	November 28
Mother's Day	December 8
Christmas	December 25

Food and Drink

There is no particular type of food that is specifically Panamanian. Instead, the restaurants and recipes come from all over—they are Chinese, African, Spanish, American.

Workers weigh fish at a market in Panama City. Popular fish eaten in Panama include red snapper and sea bass.

In the crowded cities, many restaurants are on upper floors of buildings. To serve customers at tables on the sidewalks, restaurant workers lower the food out a window to the waiters below who deliver it to the tables.

The word *Panama* originally meant "abundance of fish," so it's not surprising that fish and other seafood are staples in the Panamanian diet. Whatever the fishers catch shows up in the street markets almost immediately. Crab, lobster, and shrimp are popular, as are fish such as sea bass and red snapper. Street vendors sell *ceviche*, which is chunks of raw red snapper that has been soaked in lime juice.

The dish called *sancocho* is considered the Panamanian national dish. Originally from the Azuero Peninsula, it is chicken soup loaded with many other ingredients, such as cassava, a starchy root. It is usually served with rice and can be as spicy as a family

likes. This dish and many others are flavored with the herb cilantro. *Ropa vieja*, which translates as "old clothes," is a traditional dish of shredded beef in a sauce.

Tortillas are thin corn pancakes popular throughout Latin America, but Panama's tortillas are a bit thicker than those from other countries. Panamanians do not eat as much corn as people in many other Latin American countries do.

Most adult Panamanians start the day with coffee, which is grown in their own country. Children often drink sugarcane juice, which may come directly from a cane press. The juice can be boiled down until it becomes a thick syrup.

Panamanians relax with coffee at a café in Bocas del Toro. Panamanians typically drink their coffee mixed with sweetened milk.

Sancocho

Sancocho is a delicious chicken soup that is a staple in Panama. Have an adult help you with this recipe.

Ingredients

4 chicken drumsticks

1 tablespoon cilantro, minced

1 teaspoon dried oregano

3 garlic cloves, minced

3 teaspoons salt

2 teaspoons olive oil

1 large onion, chopped

4 cups chicken stock

3 pounds cassava, peeled and chopped

1 large ear of corn, cut into 4 pieces

Salt and pepper

Directions

Rinse the chicken pieces and pat them dry. Mix the cilantro, oregano, garlic, salt, and olive oil in a small bowl. Rub the mixture on the chicken drumsticks and let them sit for 10 minutes. Put the chicken in a large pot and cook over medium heat for about 7 minutes. Add the onion and the chicken stock. Bring the mixture to a boil, and then simmer over low heat until the chicken is cooked. Increase the heat to medium, and add the cassava and corn. Simmer until the cassava is soft, about 10 minutes. Add salt or pepper to taste. Serve with rice and enjoy!

Traveling

A network of roads, collectively called the Pan-American Highway, allows travelers to go from Prudhoe Bay, Alaska, in the northwestern part of North America, to Ushuaia, the capital of Tierra del Fuego in Argentina, at the southern tip of South America. Work on the Pan-American Highway began in 1937. Today, it goes through eighteen countries, traversing about 30,000 miles (48,000 km).

Less than half of Panama's 9,400 miles (15,000 km) of road is paved.

Colorful Red Devil buses are being replaced in Panama City by modern buses.

The biggest obstacle to completing the highway was in Panama, near the Colombian border. There, the large stretch of wetland and mountainous rain forest that makes up Darién Province prevented the building of permanent roads. This region is called the Darién Gap. By the 1970s, building roads through the region became controversial because it would damage the environment. Some vehicles can get through

To the Right

When the Pan-American Highway was being planned, it was obvious that one highway system needed everybody driving on the same side of the road. But in Panama, cars traveled on the left side of the road. That tradition was left over from the decades in which most bus drivers were originally from Great Britain, where they drive on the left. The government set about changing that in the 1930s, but the

bus companies objected because they had to revamp the side on which their doors opened. Finally, during World War II, there were so many American military vehicles in Panama, all driving on the right, that the government decreed that as of April 15, 1943, traffic would finally start driving only on the right. At 5:00 a.m. that day, all traffic in the country moved to the right side of the road.

the Darién Gap today, but they must be vehicles that can go off-road.

Not many Panamanians own cars. They are more likely to travel by bus, both in the big cities and in the countryside. For decades, buses called Red Devils have been a main method of transportation. They are old American school buses, mostly from Florida, that have been painted with murals in bright colors. They don't have set schedules, but people know they're coming by the blaring salsa music coming from them. Such buses are being phased out, though, and modern buses are now found in the streets of big cities. These buses are still not on reliable schedules, so many people call them White Devils. Panama City also has a new subway system to help people get around more easily.

A Guna woman talks on a cell phone.

Panamanians may not have many cars, but they have lots of cell phones. There are more than two phones for every Panamanian in the country. Many Indians in remote communities have access to cell phones, giving them contact with the rest of Panama for the first time. About half of Panamanians have access to the Internet. There are also TVs everywhere—on streets, in restaurants, and, of course, in shop windows. In an increasingly modern society, Panamanians have many opportunities to know what's going on in their world.

Timeline

PANAMANIAN HISTORY		WORLD HISTORY	
The first people arrive in Panama, probably from the north.	12,000–10,000 BCE		
		ca. 2500 BCE	The Egyptians build the pyramids and the Sphinx in Giza.
		ca. 563 BCE	The Buddha is born in India.
		313 CE	The Roman emperor Constantine legalizes Christianity.
		610	The Prophet Muhammad begins preaching a new religion called Islam.
		1054	The Eastern (Orthodox) and Western (Roman Catholic) Churches break apart.
		1095	The Crusades begin.
		1215	King John seals the Magna Carta.
		1300s	The Renaissance begins in Italy.
		1347	The plague sweeps through Europe.
		1453	Ottoman Turks capture Constantinople, conquering the Byzantine Empire.
		1492	Columbus arrives in North America.
Rodrigo de Bastidas becomes the first European to reach Panama.	1501 CE	1500s	Reformers break away from the Catholic Church, and Protestantism is born.
Vasco Núñez de Balboa crosses the Isthmus of Panama, becoming the first European to reach the Pacific Ocean.	1513		
Spaniards found a city on the Pacific coast that will become Panama City.	1519		
Panama becomes part of the Viceroyalty of Peru.	1567		
British pirate Henry Morgan destroys Panama City.	1671		
		1776	The U.S. Declaration of Independence is signed.
		1789	The French Revolution begins.
Panama declares its independence from Spain and joins the Republic of Gran Colombia.	1821		

PANAMANIAN HISTORY

Gran Colombia collapses; Panama joins Colombia in the Republic of New Granada.	**1830**
France begins an attempt to build a canal across Panama.	**1881**
The Republic of Colombia is formed, including Panama.	**1886**
Panama declares independence from Colombia; the United States is given control of the Canal Zone.	**1903**
The United States begins construction of Panama Canal.	**1904**
The Panama Canal officially opens.	**1914**
Anti-American riots in Panama result in the deaths of more than twenty Panamanians on what will be remembered as Martyrs' Day.	**1964**
Omar Torrijos establishes a military dictatorship.	**1968**
The United States agrees to transfer the canal to Panama on December 31, 1999.	**1977**
Omar Torrijos is killed in a plane crash; Manuel Noriega takes power.	**1981**
The U.S. military invades Panama.	**1989**
Panama gains control of the Panama Canal.	**1999**
Work begins on the expansion of the Panama Canal.	**2007**

WORLD HISTORY

1865	The American Civil War ends.
1879	The first practical lightbulb is invented.
1914	World War I begins.
1917	The Bolshevik Revolution brings communism to Russia.
1929	A worldwide economic depression begins.
1939	World War II begins.
1945	World War II ends.
1969	Humans land on the Moon.
1975	The Vietnam War ends.
1989	The Berlin Wall is torn down as communism crumbles in Eastern Europe.
1991	The Soviet Union breaks into separate states.
2001	Terrorists attack the World Trade Center in New York City and the Pentagon near Washington, D.C.
2004	A tsunami in the Indian Ocean destroys coastlines in Africa, India, and Southeast Asia.
2008	The United States elects its first African American president.

Fast Facts

Official name: Republic of Panama

Capital: Panama City

Official language: Spanish

Panama City

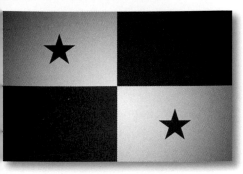

Panamanian Flag

Official religion:	None
Year of founding:	1903
National anthem:	"Himno Istmeño" ("Hymn of the Isthmus")
Government:	Constitutional democracy
Head of state:	President
Head of government:	President
Area of country:	29,120 square miles (75,420 sq km)
Greatest distance east–west:	480 miles (772 km)
Greatest distance north–south:	110 miles (177 km)
Coastline:	1,543 miles (2,483 km), including islands
Border with Costa Rica:	205 miles (330 km) long
Border with Colombia:	140 miles (225 km) long
Highest elevation:	Barú Volcano, 11,401 feet (3,475 m)
Lowest elevation:	Sea level along the Pacific Ocean
Largest lake:	Gatún, 166 square miles (430 sq km)
Longest river:	Chucunaque, 144 miles (232 km)
Average high temperature:	In Panama City, 93°F (34°C)
Average low temperature:	In Panama City, 68°F (20°C)

San Blas Islands

Casco Viejo

Currency

National population (2012 est.):	3,510,045	
Population of major cities (2010 est.):	Panama City	880,691
	San Miguelito	315,019
	Tocumen	103,117
	David	89,442
	Las Cumbres	89,000
	Colón	78,000

Landmarks:
- ▶ *La Amistad International Park*, Chiriquí and Bocas del Toro provinces
- ▶ *Casco Viejo*, Panama City
- ▶ *Gatún Lake*, near Colón
- ▶ *National Theater*, Panama City
- ▶ *Panama Canal*

Economy: Services account for about 78 percent of Panama's economy. Major service industries include running the canal, banking, the Panamanian ship registry, trade, and tourism. Major agricultural products include bananas, sugarcane, rice, and coffee. Food products, cement, and textiles are manufactured in Panama.

Currency: Panama uses U.S. dollar bills and coins called balboas, which are equal in value to U.S. currency.

System of weights and measures: Metric system

Literacy rate (2012): 94%

Schoolchildren

Rod Carew

Common Spanish words and phrases:

Por favor	Please
Gracias	Thank you
De nada	You're welcome
Sí	Yes
¡Hola!	Hello
¿Habla inglés?	Do you speak English?
No hablo español	I don't speak Spanish

Prominent Panamanians:

Rubén Blades (1948–)
Singer and actor

Alfonso Teofilo Brown (1902–1951)
First Hispanic world boxing champ

Rod Carew (1945–)
Baseball player

Mireya Moscoso (1946–)
President

Manuel Noriega (1934–)
Dictator

Laffit Pincay Jr. (1946–)
Jockey

Omar Torrijos (1929–1981)
Dictator

To Find Out More

Books

▶ Benoit, Peter. *The Panama Canal.* New York: Scholastic, 2014.

▶ Crandell, Rachel. *Hands of the Rain Forest: The Emberá People of Panama.* New York: Henry Holt, 2009.

▶ Gritzner, Charles F., and Linnea C. Swanson. *Panama.* New York: Chelsea House, 2008.

Music

▶ Los Del Azuero. *Traditional Music from Panama.* Ganarew, UK: Nimbus Records, 1999.

▶ *Music of the Indians of Panama: The Cuna.* Washington, DC: Smithsonian Folkways, 2012.

▶ Pérez, Danilo. *Panama 500.* Harper Woods, MI: Mack Avenue Records, 2014.

▶ Visit this Scholastic Web site for more information on Panama:
www.factsfornow.scholastic.com
Enter the keyword **Panama**

Index

Page numbers in *italics* indicate illustrations.

capybaras, 38
Carew, Rod, 115, *115*, 133, *133*
Caribbean Plate, 22
Caribbean Sea, 21, 22, 23, 27, 28, 117
Carnival celebration, 106, *107*, 121, *121*
Carter, Jimmy, 19, 65, *65*
Casco Viejo (Old Quarter), 72, *72*
Catholic Church, *104*
cell phones, 127, *127*
Centennial Bridge, 87, *87*
Cerro Hoya National Park, 44
ceviche (food), 122
Chagres National Park, 27
Chagres River, 15, 27, 38
Charles V, king of Spain, 49, 51
Cheucarama, Chafil, 113
children, 41, *92*, 98, *104*, 115, *118*, 119, 123
Chinese people, 94, *95*
Chiriquí Province, 29, 76, *77*, 82, 98
Chocó province, 99
Christianity. *See* Protestantism; Roman Catholicism.
Christmas holiday, 105–106
Chucunaque River, 24, 26
Church of San Pedro, 106, *106*
circuit courts, 74
cities. *See also* Colón; Panama City; towns; villages.
  Cristóbal, 85
  David, 29, 93, 108, 115
  La Chorrera, 115
  Las Cumbres, 29, 93
  San Miguelito, 29, 93
  Santiago de Veraguas, 29, *29*
  Tocumen, 29, 93
climate, 26, 30–31, *30*, 76, 82, 97, 103
clothing, 98, 102, 114, *114*
cloud forests, 43, *43*, 44
coastline, 24, 30, 117, *117*
Coclé Province, 76, *77*
cocobolo wood, 114
Cocos Plate, 22
coffee, 82, *83*, 123, *123*
Coiba Island, 28, *28*, 45

Colombia
  Chocó province, 99
  drug trade and, 65
  Emberá-Wounaan people in, 99
  government and, 11, 12–13, 54, 55–56, 57, 59
  independence from, 12–13, *13*, 14, 53, 59–60, 70
  Panama Canal Company and, 11
  Thousand Days' War, 58, *58*
  United States and, 55–56, 57, 59
Colón. *See also* cities.
  Alfonso Teofilo Brown and, 116
  architecture in, *29*
  Canal Zone and, 16, 29
  crime in, 120
  free-trade zone in, 85
  Gatún Locks, 15
  immigrants in, 94
  independence celebration in, *13*
  Islamic religion in, 107
  Jewish population, 108
  mining in, 84
  population of, 29, 93
  rebels in, 56, *56*
Colón Province, 76, *77*
Columbus, Christopher, 47, 48, *49*
comarcas indígenas (indigenous territories), 76–78, *77*, 84, 96, 98, 99
common iguanas. *See* green iguanas.
communication, 127, *127*
conga drums, 112, *112*
conquistadores (explorer-soldiers), 48, 49, 91, 109
conservation, 84
constitution, 64, 69, 70, 75, 105
Contadora Island, 28
continental divide, 23
copper mining, 83–84
coral reefs, 45, 98
coral snakes, 41
corotu trees, 35
crime, 67, 74–75, 120

criollos (Western-born Spanish people), 53
Cristóbal, 85
currency (balboas), *51*, 91, *91*

D
dams, 90–91, *90*
dancing, 106
Darién Gap, 126–127
Darién National Park, 43
Darién Province, 26, 49, 50, 76, *76*, 77, *77*, 91, 126
David, 29, 93, 108, 115
dictatorships, 64, 65–66, 69, 75, *75*, 133
diseases, 41, 49, 57, 96
dove orchid (national flower), 34, *34*
Drake, Sir Francis, 51
droughts, 31, *31*
drug trade, 65
dugout canoes, *101*, 103
Durán, Roberto, 116

E
Easter holiday, 106
economy
  agriculture and, 81
  banking industry, 29, 89
  currency (balboas), *51*, 91, *91*
  drug trade and, 65
  exports, 82, 85–86
  free-trade zones, 85, 86
  growth of, 81
  imports, 85
  logging industry, 35, *35*, 43, 82
  manufacturing, 83, 85
  mining, 48, 51, 52, 83–84, *84*, 85, 98–99, *99*
  Panama Canal and, 17–18, 81
  service industries, 81, 86
  taxes, 85, 86, 90
  tourism, 28, 29, 89, *89*, 109, 113
  trade, 47, 50, 82, 85–86
  World War II and, 18

Meet the Author

THE PANAMA CANAL WAS ONE OF JEAN BLASHFIELD'S favorite subjects from earliest childhood because her father, an engineer, frequently marveled over the amazing engineering feat of building it. Later, she found that the country surrounding the canal was just as fascinating.

Blashfield has written more than 160 books, most of them for young people. Many of them have been for Scholastic's Enchantment of the World and America the Beautiful series. She has also created an encyclopedia of aviation and space, written popular books on murderers and houseplants (not in the same book), and had a lot of fun creating a book on the things women have done called *Hellraisers, Heroines, and Holy Women*. She also founded the Dungeons & Dragons fantasy book department, which is now part of Wizards of the Coast.

Born in Madison, Wisconsin, Jean Blashfield grew up in the Chicago area and graduated from the University of Michigan. She has two grown children and three grandchildren.

Photo Credits